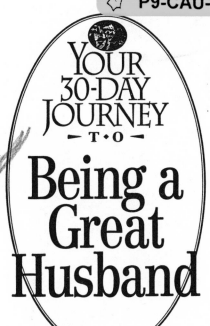

YOUR 30-DAY JOURNEY

— T • O —

Being a Great Husband

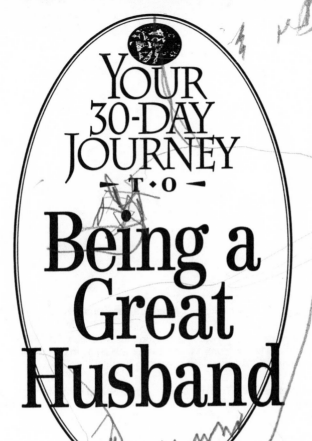

YOUR 30-DAY JOURNEY
— T·O —
Being a Great Husband

C. W. NEAL

THOMAS NELSON PUBLISHERS
Nashville

Published in Nashville, Tennessee, by Oliver-Nelson Books, a division of Thomas Nelson, Inc., Publishers, and distributed in Canada by Lawson Falle, Ltd., Cambridge, Ontario.

The Bible version used in this publication is THE NEW KING JAMES VERSION. Copyright © 1979, 1980, 1982, Thomas Nelson, Inc., Publishers.

Library of Congress Cataloging-in-Publication Data

Neal, C. W. (Connie W.). 1958-
    Your 30-day journey to being a great husband / C. W. Neal.
        p.   cm.
    ISBN 0-8407-9640-4 (pbk.)
    1. Husbands—United States.   2. Marriage—United States.
3. Marriage—Religious aspects—Christianity.   I. Title.
II. Title: Your thirty-day journey to being a great husband.
HQ756.N42   1992
646.7'8—dc20   92-27497
                                                            CIP

Printed in the United States of America
1 2 3 4 5 6 — 97 96 95 94 93 92

Contents

Introduction

In this life, you get back what you give out. If you are the kind of man who will commit your energies to bringing excellence to your role as a husband, you will get back the rare riches only an excellent marriage can give. This book is not light reading for the sake of entertainment; it's a call to action. If you are not the kind of man to take your marriage for granted, or if you have taken your marriage for granted and are starting to see the negative impact this is having on your quality of life, this book will work for you because you will be willing to work on you. Your active response to this 30-day guidebook can start the cycle that will bring back to you the kind of family relationships that supply deep satisfaction and security. These form the basis for success in all other facets of your life and work.

You can be a great husband . . . if you choose to and are willing to take the necessary steps. This book will lead you as you explore what it means to be a great husband to your wife. You will find some markers to guide you as you make choices, initiate changes, and set long-range goals that will bring results that can have a powerfully positive impact on your marriage.

Being a great husband and making the most of your marriage are ongoing processes. As you move through various stages of life, your marriage takes on new and changing qualities, requiring you to grow: in becoming the best you can be in each season of life, in love for your wife, and in your skill at partnering together. This book will guide you toward becoming the best husband you can be and planning to change and grow in ways that allow you to continue being a great husband.

If you feel that your marriage is missing something and you have fallen into the trap of blaming your wife and trying to make her change, let go of that. Your attempts to change her will probably be counterproductive. The best thing you can do is to focus on changing your own life. You will be amazed at the power of love in action to inspire your wife to respond to the positive changes in your life. If you are frustrated at trying to change your wife, give it a rest for the next 30 days and try something new. Try focusing on you.

You can't expect a total marital make-over in one month. However, if you will take the next 30 days to consider honestly what you can do in your life to be a great husband, the future course of your married life will have to take a more positive direction. This book has no power to change you until you begin to participate. Your willingness to explore life, love your wife, and try some new ways (or refresh some old ways you've forgotten) will bring about the changes you're hoping for.

P.S. If you are a wife about to buy this book for your husband, that's fine . . . as long as you also get the companion volume, *Your 30-Day Journey to Being a Great Wife* to use for yourself!

Your Commitment
to Your Journey

Every journey involves a certain amount of work, which is the energy needed to get you from here to there. This journey is no different. To get where you want to be, you will need to expend your energies and abilities in the following ways: reading, re-thinking your role and relationship, looking at yourself, changing your perspective, making new choices, changing attitudes, taking action, and reflecting on what you are learning and experiencing.

Each day's itinerary is set for you in general terms. You will make it apply to your particular situation. At every point along the way, you are free to choose your own level of involvement. You don't have to use all the information provided or do everything suggested. You may think of things not mentioned that would apply to your situation. You are free to add them to your itinerary. You move as much as *you* choose.

Completing the journey will take commitment on your part. Doing anything consistently for 30 days takes commitment, especially when you may be changing attitudes and habits. Each day's agenda will take at least 30 minutes, and you may find that you want to take more time than that, especially if you end up discussing the issues with someone. Beyond the time required, you will need to commit yourself to find courage to keep going when the personal evaluation and new ways of relating to your wife feel foreign or uncomfortable.

PERSONAL EVALUATION

Are you willing to make a 30-day commitment to your journey to being a great husband?

ACTION

My Personal Commitment

I, ___Jeff___, am serious about my desire to be a great husband to my wife, *(her name here)*___Jamie___.

I am willing to invest at least thirty minutes a day, from each of the next 30 days, to focus on this journey. I will plan to take this time each *(circle one):* morning, midday, afternoon, evening, or before bedtime.

I understand that in order to reach this goal I must be willing to grow on a personal level, to exercise the courage to look at myself honestly, and to make choices to give of myself. I will do *my* best in all of these areas.

Since my goal is to become a great husband, not a perfect husband, in the next 30 days, I will not focus my attention on how far I fall short of the ideal. I will focus my attention on *moving forward* from where I am today, toward what I want to be. I make this commitment to myself this __1__ day of ___May___, 19 ___2004___.

_____
Signature

REFLECTION

This section encourages you to reflect on each day's journey, determine how you feel about it, and look for any insight that may help you proceed. You can choose to do this by talking it over with someone, writing in a private journal, praying about it, or just taking a few quiet minutes to think about your reactions to each day's journey. Take a moment now to decide which of these means of reflection you prefer. You may want to choose a combination. There is no right or wrong way. What's important is that you do what works best to help you gain insight about your journey.

Take a few moments today to reflect on the commitment you have made and how you're feeling about beginning this journey.

ENCOURAGEMENT

Your willingness to commit yourself is the key element needed for you to be a great husband. Your choice to make this journey has already put your feet on the path to success.

FOOD FOR THOUGHT

One person with a commitment is worth one hundred who only have an interest.

—Mary Crowley

A Great Husband...
By Whose Definition?

Are you a great husband? Are you sure? Stop and consider these questions. You may find them difficult to answer because being a great husband is hard to define. You have the opportunity within the next 30 days to answer these questions with a resounding yes! You will do this by clarifying your definition of a great husband, setting specific, measurable goals, and choosing to take action to reach those goals.

Let's look at the phrase "being a great husband" and see what it involves that makes it difficult to define.

Being

Your being and identity are at the heart of your estimation of yourself. If you have a healthy self-image, you will find it easy to see yourself in positive terms whenever you consider various roles you play.

If you have a poor self-image, you may find it difficult to say you are even adequate in fulfilling the role of being a husband. A poor self-image may leave you feeling like a failure, even if your wife tells you otherwise. To have confidence that you are a great husband, you need to take steps to build a healthy self-image.

Great

In order to know something is great, you must first know what is adequate, expected, or acceptable. To have confidence that you are a great husband, you must first clarify your expectations of what is acceptable. The role of husband is changing so quickly that if you are looking to societal norms to give you a stable standard of measurement, you may find yourself on shaky ground. If you base your estimation on biblical or more traditional family guidelines, you will have a more stable standard of measurement. But you will still need to clarify your understanding of how to apply biblical principles to your life.

The measure of greatness is also dependent on whom you allow to participate in the judging. It is normal to want to please your wife. And it is normal to compare yourself to other men to get a sense of how well you are doing. You are the one who decides who sits on your panel of judges. Whom you allow to define your role as a husband will determine what being a great husband means to you.

Husband

What is a husband, anyway? The best definition of a husband I could piece together from the dictionary pointed to these central elements: a man, legally united to a woman, through an act of devotion of himself to the union.

The Bible gives God's perspective on what it means to be a husband, which goes beyond what *Webster's* has the authority to define. When a man becomes a husband, God joins him together with his wife in a spiritual union. God declared that it is not good for you to be alone. He created your wife to be your helper and you to be a covering of loving protection for her. The marriage relationship was designed to lead to the ultimate satisfaction of each partner, without either being subjugated to the other. God also assigned the husband the responsibility of being the head of the family. With this responsibility comes the command to love your wife self-sacrificially.

Being a great husband will always stay within the boundaries of fulfilling the vows you made as you entered into marriage. You, and every other husband, must carefully consider whether you can depart from the design given by the Creator of men and women, the Creator of the family, without also departing from success as a husband.

PERSONAL EVALUATION

- How does your self-image (positive or negative) affect your ability to see yourself as a great husband?
- Are you willing to take steps to improve your self-image in order to be able to be a great husband? YES
- What standard of measurement do you use as a basis for deciding whether you are a good husband or a great husband? God's? Your friend's? Society's? Your wife's?

ACTION

Use a notebook to keep a record of your 30-day journey. On the first page write out your definition of a great husband. You can use any sources you wish to help you come up with your definition.

Ask your wife to write out her definition of a great husband. Seal it in an envelope that she will hold until the end of your journey.

REFLECTION

Could you be a great husband, even if your wife never acknowledges it? If your definition of a great husband is dependent on the approval of your wife, is it really a goal you can reach?

Being a Great Husband... The Choice Is All Yours

Being a great husband is a matter of choice, and the choice is all yours. No one else can make you a great husband, and no one else can keep you from being a great husband if that is what you decide to be. It is a matter of how you choose to utilize your abilities. You can be a great husband regardless of whether or not your wife is a great wife or whether she will ever admit that you are a great husband. Her involvement can influence whether you have a great marriage, but you alone make the choices that determine whether you are a great husband.

The ingredients called for are common. You have what it takes. You have the ability to know, help, love, encourage, lend support, understand, touch, feel, express yourself, share your wisdom, affirm, appreciate, listen, evoke trust, provide a safe haven, forgive, enjoy sexual intimacy, respect, praise, honestly confront, persevere, show kindness, display affection, nurture, articulate what you need and want, and much more. It is your choice to devote these abilities to being a great husband or not.

To devote or dedicate something means to set it apart for a special purpose. When you choose to devote your life to a specific purpose, the act of devotion necessarily limits the focus of your life. Being a great husband is a matter of devotion.

Your life will be devoted to more than just being a husband. However, this act of devotion is the only one that dedicates the entire length of your life to another person. For a season of time, you will be dedicated to your children, career, and friends. But if your marriage vows are fulfilled, you will be in union with your wife for the course of this natural life, and your purpose in relationship to her will not change. Therefore, your devotion to being a husband takes preeminence.

When you chose to dedicate yourself to being a husband, to loving your wife and being her partner in life, you acted to define part of your chosen purpose for the course of your life. When you made this choice you closed the door to other women, promising to keep yourself only unto her and forsaking all others, until death. This act of devotion also calls for closing the door to other uses of your life that would interfere with your devotion in marriage. This is a commitment that needs to be guarded every time you make a choice about your priorities, the focus of your attention, and how you spend your time and energy.

PERSONAL EVALUATION

- Are you blaming anyone but yourself if you do not see yourself as a great husband?
- Are you willing to accept that you alone determine whether you are a great husband?
- To what have you devoted your life? (Being a husband, father, friend, child of God, employee, musician, artist, athlete, writer, and so on.)
- Where do you experience conflict between any of

the things to which you have devoted yourself and your primary devotion to marriage? Is there a conflict between what it takes for you to be a great husband and fulfilling your role at work or with your children? Are there other things you are devoted to that conflict with your devotion to your wife or cause confusion when you make decisions about the use of your time?

ACTION

Title a page in your notebook: The Devotion of My Life. On this page list things to which your life is devoted.

Next to each one, place a number noting its priority. Dare to be honest. Don't put your role of being a husband first just because that is the focus of this book. In your own heart, at this very moment, which of those items to which you have devoted your life mean the most to you? One way to judge relative importance is to determine which ones win out when you have to decide how to spend your time, energy, and emotional reserves.

If you want to be a great husband, choose (as an act of will) to make devotion to your wife a top priority.

REFLECTION

How does elevating devotion to your wife to a top priority limit or change your involvement in each of the other items on your list?

ENCOURAGEMENT

By making the choice to devote yourself to being a great husband, you will say no to some good things, but you will be saying yes to the best in your marriage.

FOOD FOR THOUGHT

We must not, in trying to think about how we can make a big difference, ignore the small daily difference we can make which, over time, adds up to big differences we cannot see.

—Marian Wright Edelman

Setting Goals That Lead to Being a Great Husband

This 30-day journey is a positive step forward in a journey that never ends. You may already be a great husband. If you are, this will give you a chance to polish your strengths.

This 30-day journey is a time for setting some specific short-term goals that will bring changes in your life-style. These then flow into the fulfillment of the ongoing goal of being a great husband. On day 30, when you evaluate your progress and decide where you go from here, you will be in a better position to know what obstacles you face, what skills and knowledge you need to acquire, and what help you need to reach the ongoing goal of being a great husband for life.

Your first step to setting goals that lead to being a great husband is to clearly define your objective in measurable terms. Here is a general definition you can use to help clarify your specific personal goals. Being a great husband involves your identity (being), your relationship (knowing and loving your wife), and your function (partnering with her). My idea of being a great husband is depicted in the three spheres of this diagram:

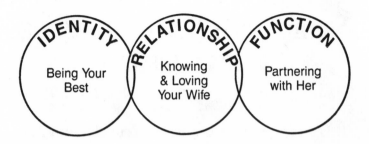

In the context of this journey you will be seeing yourself in these three primary areas: (1) becoming the best you can be, (2) strengthening your relationship with your wife by knowing and loving her, and (3) improving your partnering skills.

This book focuses on specific ways you can grow in each of these areas. You will have the opportunity to make simple changes in each area that can make a great difference in your life and marriage. You can also use your knowledge of yourself and your wife to think of other things you can do, which may not be included specifically in these categories but which you tailor to the special needs in your marriage.

PERSONAL EVALUATION

- Of the three areas in the diagram, in which area would you say you have the most room for improvement?
- In which area do you feel the most successful?
- What are a few short-term goals you could think of for each area?
- What are a few long-range goals?

ACTION

Copy this diagram into your notebook. Rate yourself on a scale of one to ten (one is poor; ten is excellent) for each sphere in terms of how well you believe you function in that category.

Make three sections in your notebook. Title them: Being My Best, Knowing & Loving Her, and Partnering in Life. On a sheet in each section list three specific short-term goals you know would help move you toward being a great husband. Also list three long-term goals that would help you in each area.

Take some action today to move toward doing one of the things you listed as a short term goal in each area. For Being Your Best you might choose something as simple as taking a brisk walk or working out at the gym. For knowing and loving your wife you might write her a love note. For partnering together with her you might ask about a problem she is facing and offer to help in some way.

REFLECTION

There are real obstacles in life when we are dealing with human relationships. Consider what obstacles stand in your way as you move toward being a great husband. What keeps you from being your best? What keeps you from knowing your wife intimately? What keeps you from loving your wife wholeheartedly? What keeps you from being a great partner?

ENCOURAGEMENT

If you continue to make daily choices to be your best, devoting yourself wholeheartedly to knowing and loving your wife and working toward the goal of being a great partner, you will be a great husband.

FOOD FOR THOUGHT

Take short steps. A lot of people fail because they try to take too big a step too quickly.

—Zig Ziglar

The Benefits of Being a Great Husband

The story is told of a man who was given the opportunity to visit both heaven and hell. When the man arrived in hell he was quite surprised by what he saw. Instead of the expected fire and brimstone, he saw an enormous banquet table about five feet wide, which extended as far as his eye could see. People were seated along each side. The banquet set before them was rich. An abundance of fruits and vegetables was elegantly arranged. The aroma of fresh baked breads and pies wafted through the air. Every imaginable type of meat, poultry, and fish, cooked to perfection, awaited the diners, along with gravies and garnishes.

At first the man was so overwhelmed by the banquet, he failed to notice the faces of the people seated there. They were pitiful, hungry, scared, desperate. When his attention turned to them, the visitor to hell was sobered by what he saw. Before each one was placed the foods they most hungered for, but no one was eating. The banquet was left untouched, although there was a great commotion around the table. A closer look revealed the reason for the commotion. Each person was unable to bend their arms to serve themselves. Splints were attached to the insides of their arms so it was impossible to bend them at the elbows. Try as they would to lift the food they craved, they could never get it to their mouths.

As the frustration mounted, people began to vent their anger on those near them. Fearing the others would take the food they wanted, they began using their outstretched arms to batter one another. This was how they would spend eternity: always seeing before them that which would feed their hunger, but never able to experience it; always fighting to make sure no one took away what they wanted, but never getting what they desperately needed.

Next, the visitor went to heaven, eager to peer behind those pearly gates. Again, he saw an enormous banquet table extending as far as his eye could see, with people seated along each side. The array of food was identical to the lavish repast he had seen in hell. Here too, each person was unable to bend their arms to serve themselves. They too were limited with splints attached to the insides of their arms so they could not bend their elbows.

But here everyone was eating. What made the difference at this table was that each one chose to serve his or her partner. The server not only enjoyed that which he was served, but also enjoyed the part he played in serving his partner. Everyone here knew that they could not nourish themselves as they needed to be nourished, but realized there was someone who cared enough for them to provide what they needed. They too knew the joy of being able to provide for another who was in need.

In this story, as in marriage, the willingness to recognize needs and extend yourself to meet those needs makes the difference between starvation and satisfaction, between frustration and fulfillment, between hell and heaven.

When you are a great husband, you extend your life

to understand and meet the needs of your wife, you serve her as a demonstration of your love for her, and you also benefit. The atmosphere of your home will improve, the intimacy of your relationship will increase, and the sense of self-respect you gain will be evident.

PERSONAL EVALUATION

- Is the atmosphere in your marriage more like the banquet table in hell or the one in heaven?
- What are the needs within your life and marriage for which you are hungry, but unable to reach on your own? Do you think your willingness to reach out to meet your wife's needs may change the atmosphere so that she would be more inclined to reciprocate?
- What benefits can you imagine receiving when you are a great husband?

ACTION

In your notebook make a list of benefits you will gain from being a great husband. Some of these will take the form of the kind of response you hope to get back from your wife when she begins to appreciate the changes you make. Be sure to list some benefits from being a great husband that are not dependent on your wife's response.

REFLECTION

Some people say that what goes around comes around, or that whatever you give out will always come back to you. The Bible says, "Give, and it will be given to you: good measure, pressed down, shaken together, and running over. . . . For with the same measure that you use, it will be measured back to you" (Luke 6:38). Imagine what could happen when you change the measure you are giving out.

ENCOURAGEMENT

There are many benefits you will receive from being a great husband. As you focus your attention on loving your wife, you will find that your own life is enriched in the process.

FOOD FOR THOUGHT

What you get by reaching your goal is not nearly as important as what you become by reaching your goal.
—Zig Ziglar

Accept Responsibility for Your Life

All forms of positive change require accepting personal responsibility for your life. As long as you abdicate responsibility for your wholeness, health, or happiness to your wife or anyone else, you will have great excuses but little power to create a better life.

When you accept responsibility you will see to it that your needs are being met from a variety of sources. When your needs are met, you will experience the kind of life that leaves you with something left over to share with others. Out of your sense of well-being you will be able to give generously to your wife. You will not have to focus on trying to make others be what you need. Instead, you will become a refreshing well from which they can draw. You will feel like giving, and be able to do so eagerly.

If you allow yourself to become depleted while waiting for someone else to meet your needs, you will end up in deficit, always demanding your way, grasping for nourishment, growing in resentment toward whoever you believe owes you what you lack. You will become the kind of person who drains those around them. When you are in this state of being you can't be a great husband, because your focus will always be on finding new ways to get someone to fill up your deficit instead of giving of yourself the way a great husband must be able to do.

Everyone needs to beware of the potential traps of irresponsibility. In marriage there is ample opportunity to shift blame for your lack of fulfillment to your wife. Below are some common traps that characterize failing to accept full responsibility for your life. Check to see if you are stuck in any of them.

Faulty beliefs

You may have grown up believing your wife would make you happy. No human being can bear responsibility for another person's feelings. Hopefully, your wife loves you in ways that enhance your enjoyment of life, but she can not bear the blame if you are not happy with yourself or your life. If you believe your wife is supposed to make you happy, a change of mind is the first step toward happiness. As long as you believe your happiness is in the hands of another, you will have no power to find the happiness you desire.

Another faulty belief is that marriage is a 50–50 proposition. Being a great husband requires accepting the understanding that each partner gives 100 percent. If you believe it's 50–50, you may continually compare your level of giving with that of your wife. If you are judging how much you will give on the basis of how much you see her giving, this shifts your full responsibility for participation in marriage off of you.

Blaming your wife

According to Ted, his wife is the source of all his problems. He wouldn't be so depressed if she took better care of him and kept the kids out of his hair. He would have gotten that promotion if she had done a better job of being the corporate wife. He wouldn't flirt with the women in his office if she were sexier. On and on it goes. To hear Ted tell the story, his wife is to blame for every failure or lack in his life. This type of blame shifting is an attempt to escape responsibility for the areas of life where you may not measure up to your own expectations. If you fall into this trap, you would do far better to face your disappointments, understand where your lack or problems lie, and deal with them directly.

When you blame your wife for every failure or lack in your own life, you lose in two ways. First, you miss being able to resolve the real problem because you don't face it. Second, you lose your wife's support in facing the problems. When she is being blamed she will probably put her energy into defending herself, rather than supporting you in your efforts to succeed in life.

Acting like a dependent child

Your wife should not take over the role Mom played when you were a boy, picking up after you, folding your underwear just the way you like it, acting as doting caretaker. If you live your life as a dependent child, you must begin the weaning process. Being a great husband requires behaving as a mature adult.

Being responsible for others

There are some men who focus their attention on fixing everyone else's lives, their wives' included, while never focusing on personal issues that need attention. Sometimes continually rescuing others is a smoke screen to keep the attention away from parts of your life that seem too painful to face.

If you want to be a great husband, accept responsibility for your life. This does not mean you become self-sufficient, pretending you don't need your wife. It means you become responsible for identifying your needs and developing a network of friendships and support connecting you to people and resources that will nourish you. Your wife is certainly a key player in meeting your needs. But your life, wholeness, health, and happiness are your responsibility, not hers.

If you see your fulfillment as your wife's responsibility, you will view any unmet need as a failure on her part. Any communication from this perspective will come across as criticism and tear her down. When you approach her with a need in this way, there is no opportunity for her to give out of love. She gives rather out of belated obligation. Once you take responsibility for your life, you can begin to appreciate how she helps meet your needs. This builds her up and gives her an opportunity to give to you as an act of love.

PERSONAL EVALUATION

- Who is responsible for your fulfillment in life?
- Do you fall into any of the irresponsibility traps?
- Are you willing to accept the powerful role of taking personal responsibility for your life?

ACTION

This exercise will allow you to accept responsibility for each general area of your life. Title five sheets of paper in your notebook with these headings: Physical life, Mental and Intellectual life, Spiritual life, Emotional life, and Financial life. For each sheet, make columns across the top with these headings: Needs, Me, My wife, Other people, Other resources.

List all of the needs you can think of in the Needs column. Place check marks in the appropriate column across the page, noting whom you look to for meeting that need. If you are depending on your wife alone to meet most of your needs, you may need to consider other possible sources. Consider what you could do to meet some of your own needs. For the needs she meets, be sure to express your appreciation.

REFLECTION

Consider how accepting responsibility for having your needs met will change your attitude toward your wife.

ENCOURAGEMENT

Being personally responsible will free you and empower you to be a great husband.

Renew Your Wholehearted Commitment

Most couples enter into marriage with a whole-hearted commitment. Even though statistics predict that 50 percent of marriages won't stand the test of time, you were probably confident that the two of you were going to make it. You said, "Till death do us part," and meant it, excitedly anticipating the life you would share. You committed yourself wholeheart-edly to marriage, for better or for worse, in sickness and in health, for richer or for poorer.

As time passes you may find that life together is not what you expected. You may discover painful se-crets you had not figured on when making your mar-riage commitment. You may suffer the death of shared dreams, have your trust severely shaken, find yourself strongly attracted to another woman, experi-ence loneliness or a lack of fulfillment. You may have to grapple with the painful aftermath of infidelity. You may have to cope with the worse instead of the better, the sickness instead of the health, and being poorer rather than richer. You may develop reserva-tions, which translate into having something less than a wholehearted commitment to the union that you promised to nurture for the rest of your life.

Being unwilling to divorce does not mean that you are wholeheartedly maintaining the commitment you made on your wedding day. Studies show that making a lifetime commitment is a primary determining factor in the success of any marriage, and you are determined to be successful. So, no matter what happens, you are in the relationship for life. But is your heart fully in the relationship, or have you withdrawn out of a need for self-protection or a desire for revenge?

The wedges between you may be valid attempts at healthy self-preservation. The way to maintain a wholehearted commitment to your wife is not by pretending things are other than what they are. The wedges between you need to be addressed individually and dissolved through concerted effort from both of you.

Whatever your marital experience, if you want to be a great husband, you need to choose your wife again today, and each day of your life. A wholehearted commitment sometimes takes courage. You can weigh your choices, and if you are going to stay in the marriage, choose to love her with your whole heart.

PERSONAL EVALUATION

- What has happened in your marriage that has caused you to hold back from wholehearted involvement? What hurts still need healing? What losses still need grieving? What betrayals still remain unforgiven? What areas of trust need to be rebuilt? What fears need to be faced and overcome?
- Do you have escape hatches prepared in case your marriage doesn't work out? How do the maintenance of these escape hatches affect your

wholehearted commitment to your marriage today?

- Are you in your marriage today because you
don't want to go through a divorce, or because
you have a wholehearted commitment to the relationship?

ACTION

In your notebook list your reservations. What you
hold back of yourself from the relationship. (This
could be sexual vulnerability, finances, kindness, information you keep from her, and so on.)

List the issues that have become wedges between
you and your wife. After each one answer yes or no
to whether the two of you can dissolve these wedges
on your own. If you have been trying without success, although you want to dissolve the wedge, you
may benefit from outside help.

Choose your wife again today. Recommit yourself
to her as an act of will, to give your marriage all you
have to offer. Choose to deal with whatever is caus-
ing you to withhold yourself.

Reaffirm your love and commitment to your wife
with words. Either tell her or write her a note to renew your commitment of love for a lifetime.

REFLECTION

Take time to look at your wedding photographs and
recall the quality of your commitment at that time.
Think of the ways your commitment was lived out
during your first year of marriage. Think of ways you
can rekindle the spirit of love your commitment took

when the relationship was young. Consider how enduring the difficulties of life together has made your mature commitment an even greater declaration of love.

ENCOURAGEMENT

By choosing her again today you will breathe fresh life and energy into your marriage.

FOOD FOR THOUGHT

A successful marriage is an edifice that must be rebuilt every day.

—André Maurois

The love we have in our youth is superficial compared to the love that an old man has for his old wife.

—Will Durant on his 90th birthday

Appreciate What You Have to Offer

Webster's gives the following definitions for the verb *appreciate:* (1) to recognize the worth of, or esteem duly; (2) to be fully conscious of; (3) to raise in value. Today you are going to appreciate yourself and what you have to offer your wife as a great husband.

To prepare a good resumé you reconsider all you have to offer: background, knowledge, experience, skills, understanding, attitude, special qualities, talents, personal attributes, special interests, and so on. You consider the requirements and purpose of the job, along with everything you know about the organization and the person making the hiring decision. A good resumé is a creative look at yourself, which is designed to convince the one doing the hiring that you are uniquely suited to the position you are seeking to fill. An effective resumé is tailored to the needs of the sought-after position.

If you have ever had to update a resumé to apply for a new position or promotion, you may have had this experience. You list all you have to offer, arrange it attractively by highlighting the particular way your qualities, abilities, and knowledge would fit the bill. When you finish and read it over, you marvel at how much you have to offer. You become fully conscious of aspects of your person and potential that may have been taken for granted by yourself and others.

You are someone special, with much to offer your wife. You have much to offer that makes you a prime candidate for being a great husband. You may be resting comfortably in the confidence that you are already hired. You may have grown bored with the assignment and continue your husbandly routine without feeling inspired to approach creatively all that being a husband can draw out of you. You may fail to realize your tremendous value as a person and what you can do in the role of husband.

PERSONAL EVALUATION

Pretend your wife has amnesia and doesn't remember her husband. She has decided to accept resumés for the position, followed by interviews for those she deems most suitable for her particular needs. Suppose there is competition and you are one of the applicants submitting a resumé for the position. You are going to reconsider yourself and what your wife needs in a husband to create a convincing resumé for the position. Below are some questions to consider in preparing the necessary information:

- What factors are of uppermost importance to her when considering her needs?
- What experience, background, knowledge, and education have prepared you for the position?
- What skills have you developed that could be utilized in the position?
- What principles and beliefs have you built your life on that give you strength?
- What personality traits and character qualities

would enable you to be a positive member of this team?
- What kind of positive difference can you make in her life if given the opportunity?
- What positive attitudes do you have that would make you attractive as someone with whom she would want to spend time?
- What demonstrates that you are trustworthy?
- How can you relate each of your qualifications to her unique needs, personality, and desires?

ACTION

Write a brief cover letter telling your wife why you want the position as her husband and request an interview.

Create a one-page resumé with the following format, filling in a paragraph for each item listed. Rework each paragraph until you feel confident that you have presented the best you have to offer in the most convincing and attractive way possible.

Your Name

Objective: Being a great husband to *(your wife's name)*_____

Education:

Experience:

Skills & Abilities:

Special Knowledge *(of her and the position):*

Personal Attributes:

Attitude:

Character Qualities:

REFLECTION

Think about what an interview for the position might be like, once your resumé is chosen. Prepare yourself mentally to answer questions that are common in job interviews such as: What are your greatest strengths and weaknesses? Why do you believe you could do this job well? How can I be sure you will stay in the position? (If your wife is agreeable, set up an appointment for an interview and see where it leads.)

ENCOURAGEMENT

By playing along with this game, you will be able to see yourself in a fresh light. You may be surprised at how much you really have to offer.

FOOD FOR THOUGHT

It's not the qualities you have. It's the qualities you recognize you have and use that will make the difference.

—Zig Ziglar

Take Care of Your Health and Appearance

When you take care of yourself physically you are demonstrating love for yourself and your wife. Although you want her to love you for the person inside, the way you treat your body is a reflection of who you are inside and your level of self-respect. Taking care of your health also has a direct influence on how long you may be around to be a husband!

There are many sensible reasons to take care of your health and appearance as it relates to being a husband. Here are some:

- Many women are now working outside the home. If your wife is one of them, she is probably surrounded by men in business settings who are attractively groomed.
- If you look better and feel better physically, you can't help but feel better about yourself. A good self-image will make you more confident in the marriage relationship.
- Good health will give you more energy to devote to the relationship.
- Looking your best will help your wife be proud of you.
- Letting your wife know that you are looking your best for her enjoyment can be a boon to your love life.

- When you are feeling fit and attractive, sexual intimacy is more appealing and enjoyable.

Here are some basic ways to take care of your health and appearance.

Exercise

For the sake of your sex life alone (not to mention your general health and well-being), take advantage of motivational material available to get you up and moving.

Sleep

Giving yourself the rest you need is a service to yourself and your wife. You must have enough sleep on a regular schedule if you are to function at your peak. Lack of sleep can leave you irritable, fatigued, mentally impaired, and emotionally vulnerable.

Nutrition

Eating a nutritious diet is an important part of being a great husband.

Preventive health care

Taking care of your health is a way of showing your love to your family. If you maintain a regular routine of preventive health care, you will be sick less often. Since early detection is crucial to the survival rate among people with many types of cancer and heart disease, your commitment to preventive health care may mean the difference between your wife's having you by her side to a rich old age or her becoming a widow.

Good physical hygiene

Keeping your body, hair, teeth, skin, and nails clean and well groomed affects the appearance and fragrance you bring to the world. It is important to care for yourself in ways that make you someone nice to be near.

Dressing up

Take care to dress attractively, in clothes that are neat, clean, stylish, and appropriate to the occasion and in colors that best display your good looks. When you dress up, you feel more attractive and are more attractive.

PERSONAL EVALUATION

- Do you get enough exercise and rest to be at your best each day?
- Is your diet nutritious and health preserving?
- Do you practice good grooming habits on a daily basis?
- Do you dress up as well for your wife as you dress up to present yourself to people you associate with outside your home?

ACTION

Rate yourself on a scale of one to ten for how well you take care of yourself in each of the following areas: exercise, sleep, nutrition, preventive health care, physical hygiene, dressing up, and grooming (one is poor; ten is excellent).

Choose three specific things you are willing to

change in your lifestyle to take better care of your health and appearance. You do not need to choose the three areas where you feel you need the most improvement; in fact, that may be self-defeating. Instead, make a commitment to make three small changes that are within your immediate reach. List in your notebook these three items in the form of a commitment. Tell someone who will be supportive of you and ask them to hold you accountable to maintain these simple changes for the next twenty-one days.

If you have not had a physical checkup in the past year, call today and make an appointment.

REFLECTION

The inability to care for yourself in these basic ways may indicate deeper problems that are affecting you and your marriage. Consider the ways you find most difficult to take care of yourself and ask yourself what the obstacles are to your health and well-being. If you can't figure it out or resolve the problem, seek professional help from someone who can assist you.

ENCOURAGEMENT

Your willingness to make positive changes in self-care will give you immediate results and make the rest of your journey more enjoyable. Do the best you can to be good to yourself.

Be Prepared to Lay Down Your Life

In the movie *Patriot Games*, the lead character, Jack Ryan, is fighting to protect his wife and child from a terrorist who is determined to destroy them, as an act of revenge against him. The driving force behind the character's willingness to risk his life is his all-consuming desire to protect his family. His wife is a strong character in her own right. In her profession as a surgeon, and in relationship with her husband, you can see she is no shrinking violet. At one point in the movie, when the threat has become deadly serious, she says to her husband, "He's never going to let us be, is he?" She knows the answer is negative. She leans her head against his shoulder and says, "Get him." The rest of the story is her husband's fight to do just that. Near the end of the movie, Jack Ryan acts as a decoy to lure the aggressor away from his family. He becomes a living example of a man willing to lay down his life for his family.

Chances are good that you'll never have to protect your wife from death threats by a zealous terrorist, nor will she probably call on you to slay dragons on her behalf. Nevertheless, a great husband must be willing to lay down his life sacrificially for his wife. The Bible says, "Husbands, love your wives, just as Christ also loved the church and gave himself for it." How did Christ love the church? Primarily, His love was demonstrated by laying down His own life as a means of protection for anyone who would come under His covering. He became a shield, a fortress, a stable rock to rely on for shelter in the daily battles of life. A husband's love is to be characterized by a similar kind of self-sacrifice.

PERSONAL EVALUATION

The following are some ways you can act to protect your wife in the common occurrences of life. Ask yourself how well you are displaying your love by doing these things. Note any of these areas where you are leaving your wife unprotected.

- Do you have adequate life and health insurance to protect and provide for your family in the event of accidents, death or other potential disaster?
- Do you have an up-to-date will that is designed with the protection of your wife and children in mind?
- Do you protect your wife from attack? Sometimes the most prevalent form of attack will come from those closest to home. Do you act as a buffer between your wife and children when the children are disrespectful to her? Do you let others in your extended family (your parents, in-laws, siblings) know that you will not tolerate any form of attack against your wife?
- Do you work to provide for your family's material needs?
- Do you provide objective feedback in decision making? When your wife is setting priorities, do

you help her weigh how each commitment will impact the rest of the family? Do you help her set boundaries and encourage her to say no, when to say yes would not be in her best interests or serve your common purposes?

- Do you set the standard for health and safety in your home? Do you set the example and family policy to ensure living in your home is safe? This would include things like always wearing seatbelts, not smoking, not drinking to excess, securing your home, establishing emergency procedures to be followed in case of fire, earthquake, or other potential danger, educating your children in personal safety skills, and so on.

- Do you have a personal problem that is out of control? If you are struggling with addiction to pornography, drugs, alcohol, gambling, or work, have other compulsive behaviors, or cannot control your rage, jealousy, or depression, the result will be that your family is left vulnerable to the consequences of your out-of-control behavior. Take care of personal problems that have a negative impact on your wife and family. If this problem continues unabated, what are the potential dangers it poses for your family?

ACTION

Look over the items listed above in the personal evaluation section and make two lists. On one list, note everything you do as an act of self-sacrifice or to protect your wife. On the second list, note everything you have not done that leaves your wife and family unprotected in some way.

Make a third list, consisting of goals derived from taking action on the items listed on the second list. For each item on the second list, turn the missing action into a goal of something you can do. For example: You may notice that you are not sure your insurance is up to date with the needs of your family. You noted on your second list: Inadequate insurance. On your third list you would write the goal: Make an appointment with the insurance agent to update our coverage.

Plan to integrate the accomplishment of the goals on your third list into the other goals of your life.

REFLECTION

How can your willingness to protect your wife serve to help her be her best? If you have ever seen your wife and family suffer because of a situation where you left them unprotected, do you still feel guilty? If so, talk this over with your wife.

ENCOURAGEMENT

The desire to protect your wife and family is already within you. Don't be afraid to acknowledge that part of you and put it into action on behalf of your family.

FOOD FOR THOUGHT

Greater love has no one than this, than to lay down one's life for his friends.

—Jesus Christ

Dare to Lead with Love

A recent news broadcast recounted the story of a family on a rafting trip that turned tragic. A husband and wife, along with their four children, took a day trip on a river. The county was responsible for clearing the river of debris, but due to a budget crunch they decided to forego the usual cleanup. The family's raft snagged on a fallen tree and was overturned. The father, mother, and two of the children were rescued safely. But the two youngest children, girls ages five and two, drowned. The father brought a lawsuit against the county for negligence, in failing to clear the trees from the river. In response, the county brought charges of negligence against the father because they claimed that the girls who drowned did so because their life jackets were not secured properly. They saw this as the father's responsibility.

Beyond the heart-wrenching tragedy of the situation, what caught my attention was the fact that although both husband and wife were aboard the raft, the proposed lawsuit was aimed at the man. Although our societal roles have changed recently, the question of ultimate responsibility for family care still is directed to the man as the head of his home. To be a great husband, a man must take personal responsibility for the care of his family.

You can be a confident leader of your family if you are willing to accept the responsibility. If all members of your family are to function well and achieve their best in life, you need to commit yourself to exercising leadership within the family. Leadership is not some mystical quality inherent in the lives of men who seem to be natural leaders. Leadership is something you can develop if you dare. When you dare to lead with love, you will create an atmosphere of security and confidence in which your wife and children can find freedom and encouragement to achieve their highest potential.

The best leaders deeply respect the value and abilities of each person in their organization. Leaders are required to make decisions that will not please everyone yet work for the good of all in achieving common objectives. The choices they make will shape and limit the options available for those under their leadership. Leaders learn to delegate, follow up on the progress of those they lead, and encourage individual excellence. Leaders also must be accountable and held responsible for their actions. They must be willing to make sacrifices for the ultimate good of those they lead.

PERSONAL EVALUATION

- Do you dare to take the responsibility for the care of your family?
- Are you and your wife in agreement regarding the authority structure of the family?
- Have you ever been accused of abusing your authority?
- Is your leadership framed in the setting of self-sacrificial love?

ACTION

In your notebook draw an organizational chart which shows lines of authority and who is currently in submission to whom within your family. Then draw an organizational chart showing how the family authority should be run, with you at the head.

Hold a family meeting to explain clearly your position of authority within the family and how your leadership will benefit everyone. Make sure each one understands his or her position and what is required of them in relationship to the others.

REFLECTION

Have members of your family ever been the victims of the abuse of authority? What beliefs might you be encountering that would make you or your family feel uncomfortable with announcing yourself as head of your family?

ENCOURAGEMENT

Leadership can be learned. By taking the time to study and consider your leadership role, you can learn to be a competent and loving leader, which is one facet of being a great husband.

FOOD FOR THOUGHT

You do not lead by hitting people over the head—that's assault not leadership.
　　　　　　　　　—Dwight D. Eisenhower

Dump the Woman of Your Dreams

While going through premarital counseling, one couple discovered the husband-to-be didn't have a clue about the true identity of the woman he was about to marry. As a part of the counseling process, Donald and Anita took the Taylor-Johnson Temperament Analysis Inventory. This questionnaire asks about how you would act and feel in various situations. You answer each question twice—once for how you would act and once for how you anticipate your partner would act. The results are plotted on a graph describing various temperament qualities on a continuum between opposite poles (like *introverted* and *extroverted*). Then the counselor superimposes the results of what you think your partner is like with what the test reveals she is really like in terms of how she says she would act in real-life situations. Donald was shocked to see that although Anita had predicted his response to life with amazing accuracy, his view of what Anita was like bore no noticeable resemblance to the real woman. The counselor spent some time helping Donald see that if his marriage were going to work, he would need to dump the woman of his dreams, learning to know and accept the woman he was about to marry.

Many men think they know the woman they marry, only to find that when the honeymoon is over, they wake up to the realization she is quite different from the woman they thought they married. Your image of your wife will need to be altered if you have superimposed your childhood dreams of what you hoped for in a wife, over the real woman. When you have an image of an ideal wife firmly envisioned in your mind, it's easy to see the real woman in that image, as you would like her to be.

When you discover the difference between the woman of your dreams and the real woman you married, you have a choice to make. You can continue to measure her against your ideal, comparing her to what you had always hoped for in a wife and trying to transform her by sheer willpower and determination. Or you can dump the woman of your dreams, enjoy the adventure of getting to know and love the real woman you married, and learn to accept and appreciate the unique human being God created her to be.

If you insist on measuring her against your fantasy, you will depreciate her unique personality and special qualities. You'll see what she is not and miss all that she is. That is a tremendous loss.

PERSONAL EVALUATION

- Do you find yourself noticing what disappoints you about your wife more than what you appreciate about her?
- Do you like your wife for who she is?
- Do you find that you are often surprised by her choices and actions?
- Do you have a hidden agenda of how you want to mold your wife into the woman of your dreams?

ACTION

Make a list of all the ways you would like to change your wife if it were in your power to do so. Put a check next to the items you actively try to change in her.

Look at each item on your list and decide if you are willing to release the responsibility for change in that area back to your wife. If so, cross that item off your list. For the items remaining on your list, ask yourself why you refuse to accept your wife as she is. What does it threaten in you? Consider discussing these issues with a marriage counselor if these are recurrent areas of contention within your marriage.

Choose to dump the woman of your dreams and give up your crusade to change your wife into your image of wifely perfection. Instead focus on getting to know and like her for who she is.

Play this game to help you discover how well you know the real woman you are committed to loving. Write your answer to each of the following questions. Once you have finished, ask your wife to answer the questions and see how well you know the real woman you married.

- What is your wife's favorite food, color, TV show, political figure, clothing outfit?
- What are three actions that speak love to her?
- What was the happiest day of her life? the saddest day?
- If she could, what would she change about her appearance, her past, her job, her marriage, her home?

- What three concerns or worries are uppermost in her mind at the moment?
- What project is she currently focused on at work (in or out of the home)?
- What does she consider her greatest personal strength and weakness?
- What talents does she have that are not currently being used as much as she would like?
- What does she feel most guilty about?
- What are three of her favorite interests or hobbies?
- What special recognition has she received or award has she won? What does she believe deserves recognition that she has not been recognized for?
- What are her religious beliefs about heaven and hell, the character of God, how God sees her, sin and forgiveness?
- What are the five most severe losses she has experienced in her life?
- What would she want written on her tombstone?

REFLECTION

Telling your wife you like her is very different from saying you love her but is every bit as important. How do you let her know you like her, as well as love her?

If you have depreciated the real woman you married by negatively comparing her to some ideal, consider whether an apology is in order.

FOOD FOR THOUGHT

This is one of the miracles of love: It gives . . . a power of seeing through its own enchantments and yet not being disenchanted.

—C. S. Lewis

Be Considerate, Kind, and Affectionate

Little things can make a big difference in a marriage. It is not just what you do in day-to-day life, but how you do it that will convey love to your wife. The little niceties of life can be grouped into three general categories: consideration, kindness, and affection. Each of these is not difficult to put into practice, but will make a big difference.

Being considerate simply means that you consider her as a unique individual, with particular likes and dislikes, with other influences she's contending with in the course of life. The way you speak, put your clothes in a hamper, dress, or make her a cup of tea, can all speak volumes of love when she realizes you chose to do it in the way she likes, being considerate of her preferences. Whenever you consider what she is going through at the moment and do something to anticipate her needs or feelings, you are being considerate.

In his book *My Little Church Around The Corner*, Randolph Ray noted, "Kindness is the life's blood, the elixir, of marriage. Kindness makes the difference between passion and caring. Kindness is tenderness. Kindness is love. . . . Kindness is good will. Kindness says, 'I want to make you happy.' Kindness comes very close to the benevolence of God."

Kindness can become a good habit in your home.

It is said that familiarity breeds contempt. There is danger in the everyday routines of marriage of allowing familiarity to diminish the kindness you show your wife. You can be kind if you focus your attention in that direction. Being kind can be as simple as trying to be nice, being gentle and tender with her, using good manners. It is an act of kindness to say please and thank you and I'm sorry. You can choose to soften the rough spots when you hold your tongue or give her the benefit of the doubt.

Being affectionate is a matter of displaying your love with a gentle touch. A warm hug, the brush of your hand across hers, an unexpected kiss, running your fingers through her hair, or a pat on the back can display your genuine affection. If you find romance to be waning, start displaying non-sexual touches of affection. These can help get the sparks of romance going again.

PERSONAL EVALUATION

- What do you do in a special way, just because you know your wife prefers it?
- How do you show her kindness?
- What kind of manners are used in your home and in relationship with your wife?
- Do you treat her with the same degree of kindness and courtesy you would show a business associate or a guest?
- In the course of the day how many times do you touch her affectionately?
- If you are not considerate, kind, and affectionate as a matter of practice, are you willing to begin practicing this way of relating?

ACTION

Focus your attention today on being considerate in the way you do things with and for your wife, practice being kind, and touching her affectionately. Don't tell her about the assignment. Take note of how different this is from your usual behavior and what kind of response comes back from her as you treat her this way.

REFLECTION

How did you feel about making these types of expressions of love? Awkward? Fearful of rejection? Loving? Happy with yourself? Do you believe you must *feel* like being kind, considerate, and affectionate before it can be genuine to act in these ways? When you began to act in these ways, did the feelings follow your actions?

ENCOURAGEMENT

Your choice to be continually considerate, kind, and affectionate will be rewarded by your feeling more loving toward your wife and better about yourself.

FOOD FOR THOUGHT

I would like to have engraved inside every wedding band, "Be kind to one another." This is the Golden Rule of marriage and the secret of making love last through the years.

—Randolph Ray

Water the Seeds of Greatness Within Her

Every woman has seeds of greatness within her. A great husband takes note of where these seeds are buried and waters them until they grow to become apparent to everyone and begin bearing fruit.

Just as seeds are buried under mounds of dirt, the seeds of good character qualities in a woman may be buried under mounds of a different kind of dirt. The seeds of honesty may be buried under feelings of inadequacy and the fear of being rejected as she truly is. The seeds of kindness may be buried under her perceived need for strong walls of defensiveness. The willingness to work hard and the ability to achieve may be just beneath the surface of past failures and discouragement. Loyalty may have been trampled in the dirt of betrayal, hidden beneath a mistrust of others. Intelligence may be under the rock of a belief, drilled into her as a child, that she is unintelligent.

You can water the seeds of greatness within her in these ways:

Assume that she has great potential and good character qualities that can be developed.

Discover what may be burying the seeds of greatness in her life. What beliefs does she hold that keep her down? What hurts has she experienced which cause her to doubt herself or others? Where has she tried and failed in the past? What conclusion is she drawing about herself on the basis of the dirt she has experienced in life?

Notice good qualities in seed form. If she tells you the truth when it would have been easier to evade the truth or misrepresent it, let her know that you appreciate her honesty. If she tries at something, even though she may not get the hoped for results, praise the strength of her effort and what she did right. If she thinks she is stupid, take note of her intelligence in action and comment on it. Mention the smart choices she makes and comment on her wise perceptions.

Water her seeds of greatness with words of encouragement. Tell her she can grow and change for the better in ways she wants to grow. Tell her you believe in her and her ability to learn new ways of life. Tell her you know she has what it takes, her talents are worth developing, her love will be received and reciprocated, her hard work will pay off in time, her failures and disappointments are cobblestones on the path to ultimate success.

Although personal growth will be the outcome of watering the seeds of greatness within her, be careful not to use this as a tactic to try to manipulate her into changing in the ways you want her to change. Be careful to note honestly what you see within her as a unique individual, rather than making things up that you would like in your ideal wife.

PERSONAL EVALUATION

- Do you assume your wife has seeds of greatness within her?
- Do you water those seeds with words of encour-

agement, or plow them under with words of criticism?

- What is some of the dirt of life you suspect may be burying the seeds of greatness within your wife?

ACTION

Title a sheet of paper: Seeds of Greatness Within My Wife. On the left side list positive qualities, talents, abilities, and potential you see in your wife. Across the page, on the right side, cite one example of how you have seen this in seed form within her life. Keep going until you have at least ten items on the page.

Look for opportunities when you can take note of, comment on, and encourage these seeds of greatness within her. As opportunities arise naturally, water the seeds of greatness you have listed by mentioning what you notice to your wife and telling her what you think is so great about her.

REFLECTION

Think about a time when your belief in your wife and your encouragement of her gave her the courage to grow. Consider how your attitude about her either can nourish positive growth or stamp it out.

ENCOURAGEMENT

It is wonderful to realize that you play a major role in helping bring out the best within your wife. Don't let a critical attitude keep you from seeing her grow into the woman she was meant to be.

FOOD FOR THOUGHT

Marriage is a partnership in which each inspires the other, and brings fruition to both.
—Millicent Carey McIntosh

Recognize Her Work, Give Some Recognition

In spite of much talk these days about sharing the load with household chores, there is still inequity in the distribution of work in many families. Often when the wife takes outside employment, her husband may still assume she can carry the same load as before.

A great husband will give his attention to what his wife's workload really entails, physically, mentally, emotionally, and psychologically. He will make a point of recognizing how much she is carrying. Perhaps you are hesitant about considering this issue in great detail for fear that you might be held responsible to help more than you are prepared to. If you recognize that your wife is bearing more than her fair share of the work, together you can plan ways to lighten the load.

Your wife needs your recognition. This can be a great encouragement to what otherwise can become a thankless job. If you disregard being attentive to her contributions, or if you belittle them in your mind just to maintain the status quo, you do her a disservice by not giving her the recognition she deserves. If you dare to look honestly at all the things your wife does, you may find that part of your display of love in your home is demonstrated by sharing more of the work of keeping your home running in an orderly manner. You may find that your wife doesn't want you to help more, but just truly to appreciate her and recognize the value of her work to the well-being of your family.

PERSONAL EVALUATION

Play this game to help you recognize how much your wife really does. Pretend that your wife will be going in for surgery that will leave her temporarily unable to move. You have to take note of everything she does in the course of the coming week, so that you can either take over doing those things yourself or find someone else to whom you can delegate those jobs. Once you have a clear idea of what her workload consists of (be sure to include getting up in the middle of the night with children if this is a regular occurrence), mentally consider what your life would be like if you had to take over her responsibilities for just one week.

ACTION

Write out a detailed description of what your wife does in the course of one week. Break the week down into hourly segments and list everything she does.

Ask your wife how she really feels about the division of labor in your home, and listen attentively.

Make needed adjustments to help your wife carry the workload of managing the home. If those duties are more than her fair share, offer to take on more yourself or agree to hire help.

Give her recognition verbally. Perhaps you might

want to give some other tangible form of appreciation.

REFLECTION

How does your preconceived notion of what a wife is supposed to do around the house insulate you from appreciating and recognizing how much she really does? Did this exercise make you feel defensive? If so, why?

ENCOURAGEMENT

Your willingness to give your wife recognition will have a tremendous impact on your marriage and home life.

FOOD FOR THOUGHT

It is estimated that it takes nine compliments to outweigh one negative comment or criticism.

Choose to Go Beyond Her Expectations

Every woman brings expectations into the marriage of what her husband is supposed to do for her. She may have even had dreams of you being her Prince Charming. Even if she doesn't expect you to help her live happily ever after, there are specific things she does expect. In every marriage there is the ongoing negotiation of expectations between husband and wife. At times, fulfilling her expectations and giving her what she wants, in the way she wants it, may be what is required.

Even though these expectations may be something rather trivial, such as keeping the top on the toothpaste or picking up your clothes, you may bristle at the thought that you have to do something a certain way just because she wants it. Human nature tends to rebel against being made to conform to the demands of others. A request opens the opportunity for free choice. Demands and expectations place you under another person's control.

In every marriage, husbands and wives will make certain demands of one another. When this happens you don't have to resent this and grudgingly give in to her demands. You can still maintain your freedom of choice and a positive attitude by choosing to go beyond your wife's expectations.

Here's the example to follow. In Palestine, at the time of Christ, the nation of Israel was occupied by the Roman army. Law dictated that any Roman soldier could demand a Jew to carry his belongings for as far as one mile. Most Jews rebelled against this symbol of subserviency and would only go grudgingly a mile with a soldier under threat of severe punishment. Jesus taught His followers to go beyond expectations. He suggested the revolutionary idea that they go a second mile, of their own free will, once the soldier's demands were met. This determination to display love by going the second mile changed their attitude. The second-mile intention turned their first-mile attitude from a grumble to a grin. The first mile they were slaves; the second mile they became lovers. The first mile the soldier was in control; the second mile they were.

You can apply this same powerful principle to your marriage by choosing to go beyond your wife's expectations. When you accept your wife's expectations and creatively plan to fulfill and exceed them, you will never feel subservient. You can stop grumbling and start grinning as you choose to display second-mile love to your wife.

PERSONAL EVALUATION

- What expectations did your wife bring into marriage about what you are supposed to do for her?
- Which of these expectations do you fulfill but do so grudgingly?
- Are you willing to make the choice to go beyond her expectations?

ACTION

Divide a sheet of paper into two columns. Write the headings First Mile in the left column and Second Mile in the right column. List ten items under First Mile that your wife expects of you. Under Second Mile think of a creative way you can fulfill her expectations and dramatically exceed them.

Pick three of these items and commit yourself to going beyond her expectations with a positive and loving attitude. Don't announce your intentions, just do it and note her response. Also notice how your feelings change as you practice going the second mile.

REFLECTION

Imagine yourself doing each of the ten items in your second-mile list. Imagine the possible change in your attitude and the atmosphere of your home.

ENCOURAGEMENT

Practicing second-mile love can make your life and marriage much more enjoyable. Try this way of life for a while and see for yourself the positive difference it can make.

FOOD FOR THOUGHT

Grumbling is the death of love.
                                    —Marlene Dietrich

Love talked about can be easily turned aside, but love demonstrated is irresistible.

—W. Stanley Mooneyham

Respond to the Differences Between You

In his book *His Needs, Her Needs: Building An Affair Proof Marriage*, William F. Harley, Jr., Ph.D., observes that men and women have two distinct sets of needs they expect their spouses to meet. In his extensive counseling experience he has noticed that failing to understand and accommodate the differing needs of your marriage partner tends to undermine any marriage. Men and women need to understand the differences between them and learn to respond to their spouses' needs rather than reacting against them.

According to Dr. Harley, the man's five most basic needs in marriage are sexual fulfillment, recreational companionship, an attractive spouse, domestic support, and admiration. The woman's five most basic needs in marriage are affection, conversation, honesty and openness, financial support, and family commitment.

He goes on to note, "If the needs of men and women are so different, no wonder they have difficulty adjusting in marriage. A man can have the best intentions to meet his wife's needs, but if he thinks her needs are similar to his own, he will fail miserably."

Responding to the differences between you involves first understanding and accepting that there are differences, then choosing to adapt your life-style to meet the needs of the woman you married. When you begin to respond positively to her as a woman, you will find a greater willingness on her part to respond to your needs. You can't treat her like one of the guys without diminishing the positive spark that attracted you to one another.

God created humankind male and female, with unique differences built in by design. The physical differences are obvious. Recent research also has highlighted differences in the way men and women think, perceive, and communicate. Beyond these general differences between you as men and women there are also many differences or opposites in your personalities. You can build your relationship by appreciating and accommodating these differences.

PERSONAL EVALUATION

- Looking at the two lists of men's and women's marital needs, have you noticed that you may be trying to satisfy in your wife needs that are more important to you than to her?
- Looking at the list of women's marital needs, what have you heard your wife say that expresses any of these needs in her life?
- What opposites of personality and temperament originally attracted you to your wife?

ACTION

Rate yourself on a scale of one to ten (one being poor; ten being great) for how well you think you fulfill each of the items most women consider priority needs in marriage.

Show your wife the lists of men's and women's marital needs. Ask her to comment on whether those needs are representative of needs she feels are important; listen carefully to what she has to say. Ask her to rate your fulfillment of these needs on a scale of one to ten. If your self-rating is different from what your wife perceives, you need to set some specific goals to help you focus more clearly on meeting the needs she finds important.

Make a list of the notable differences between you and your wife. For each item on the list note how your differences can enhance your life together.

REFLECTION

Does understanding some of the differences between you seem to relate to any area of conflict in your marriage that previously didn't make sense to you? How can accepting the differences between you enrich your marriage?

ENCOURAGEMENT

Your willingness to accept the differences between you will allow you to complement one another in ways that make life better for each of you.

FOOD FOR THOUGHT

What counts in making a happy marriage is not so much how compatible you are but how you deal with incompatibility.

—George Levinger

Practice Forgiveness

"Can you ever forgive me?" This is a very important question. If you do not learn to understand and practice forgiveness, you cannot maintain a healthy marriage. A great husband must learn to practice forgiveness for two important reasons: everyone needs to be forgiven, and a man who refuses to practice forgiveness will destroy his own well-being. No man or woman is perfect. In the course of life you and your wife will fail one another, sometimes in small ways, perhaps in major ways. Forgiveness brings reconciliation, displays love, and frees the heart from bitterness.

Misconceptions about forgiveness can convince you that forgiving your wife for some things is impossible. Let's clear away some common misconceptions so you can begin practicing forgiveness.

To forgive does not require you to suppress or disguise the feelings generated by the offense. Troubled feelings are valid even after you have chosen to forgive. Being forgiven does not excuse either of you from having to face the consequences of their actions.

To forgive does not mean you shield your wife from the natural consequences of what she has done. You may say, "Well, I forgive her. I love her. I don't want her to suffer." You can forgive her and still stand back and allow her to face responsibility for the consequences of what she has done.

To forgive doesn't mean you forgive and forget, once and for all. Forgiveness is a choice you make over and over again. You may choose to forgive today and tomorrow be tempted to hold a grudge.

Forgiveness does not excuse wrong behavior. You may believe that if you forgive your wife, that will convey that her wrongful actions were acceptable. Forgiveness pardons that which you believe to be wrong, it does not mean you pretend wrong is right.

Forgiveness involves letting go of your personal resentments and bitterness. One way to release these is to acknowledge and vent your true feelings, rather than trying to pretend that you feel fine. When you have been hurt, deceived, wronged, or betrayed, you don't feel fine. It will take time, but you can begin by determining to continue in the process until you experience the freedom forgiveness gives.

PERSONAL EVALUATION

- Somewhere in your mind there might be a list of all the offenses your wife has committed against you. Are you keeping account of every wrong suffered?
- Have you been pretending she can do no wrong because you hesitate to honestly recognize her failings?
- Do you stuff true feelings that arise in reaction to some wrong on her part because you believe that if you truly forgive her you are no longer entitled to your feelings?
- Are you able to take responsibility for your life regardless of how your wife behaves toward you?

ACTION

Today you will attempt to forgive your wife in your heart and mind for the things you have against her. If you already have been practicing forgiveness, the list may be quite short. If you have never done this, you may have a long list.

Make a list of your wife's failings, including commitments she has broken, things she did that should not have been done, and things she should have done but didn't. For each one, acknowledge the validity of the pain they cause in your life. For each item, list the consequences that are the result of wrong behavior. Recognize that forgiveness does not require you to protect her from these consequences.

Once you complete this checklist, take it before God and pray something like this:

Dear God,
Here is the list of offenses that I have been holding against my wife. Thank You that You respect our lives enough to recognize the need for accountability for these kinds of hurtful acts and omissions. I don't want to hold on to these anymore. I will give them over to You and trust that You and she can work out any further arrangements. Amen.

REFLECTION

No one is perfect. Everyone needs forgiveness from God, and from others. Remember, the measurement that you use to judge your wife will be used to measure your life. Don't let your life and marriage fall victim to unforgiveness.

ENCOURAGEMENT

It will take courage to forgive, and lots of practice, but this is something you can learn.

FOOD FOR THOUGHT

When you forgive somebody else you accept the responsibility for your own future.

—Zig Ziglar

To keep your marriage brimming,
with love, in the loving cup,
whenever you are wrong admit it,
whenever you're right, shut up.
—Ogden Nash

Practice Good Communication Skills

"I know you believe you understand what you think I said, but I'm not sure you realize that what you heard is not what I meant." This comment, from an anonymous source, exemplifies how complicated simple communication can become, even when you are doing your best to understand. All good communication takes practice and skill. In developing good communication between husband and wife there is another element that comes into play, making the process even more of a challenge. This added element is the need to understand the frame of reference from which your spouse interprets what you are saying.

In the best-seller *You Just Don't Understand: Women and Men in Conversation,* Dr. Deborah Tannen, Ph.D., says, "Talk between women and men is cross-cultural communication." She explains that because men and women engage the world in different ways, they also use words differently. Neglecting to take the differing communication styles into account may leave you both hurt and bewildered, even though each of you did your best to communicate clearly and understand what the other was trying to say.

Dr. Tannen notes that a man engages the world "as an individual in a hierarchical social order in which he was either one-up or one-down. In this world, conversations are negotiations in which people try to achieve and maintain the upper hand if they can, and protect themselves from others' attempts to put them down and push them around. Life, then, is a contest, a struggle to preserve independence and avoid failure."

In commenting on the way many women communicate, she writes that a woman engages the world "as an individual in a network of connections. In this world, conversations are negotiations for closeness in which people try to seek and give confirmation and support, and to reach consensus. They try to protect themselves from others' attempts to push them away. Life, then, is a community, a struggle to preserve intimacy and avoid isolation. Though there are hierarchies in this world too, they are hierarchies more of friendship than of power and accomplishment."

A common example of the kind of frustrations that arise from not understanding these differing perspectives may occur when your wife tries to share her feelings about a problem with you. She is looking for intimacy, closeness, and support. She wants to know you are with her, to hear your confirmation that her troubled feelings are valid. If you share the perspective many men have, where life is a contest, you may see her problem as a challenge to be conquered. She shares feelings, in hopes of greater closeness. You respond with a solution to fix the problem and thus win the contest.

Once you have offered the solution, you expect discussion to be over. The problem is solved, end of conversation. But she didn't want you to solve it; she wanted you to share it. When she continues the conversation, without accepting your advice, you may be offended that she has rejected your solution. By your way of thinking, her ongoing talk of how she is feeling about the problem may come across as a demonstration that you failed in your attempt to fix things. If she would only accept your solution to the problem, she wouldn't have to go on feeling badly. By her way of thinking, your simple dismissal of her feelings (just because there is a solution) serves to disconnect her from you.

Sharing a problem your wife feels deeply about is an opportunity for intimacy. A great husband will learn to be a good cross-cultural communicator. You can do this by educating yourself about the differences between male and female communication, and by practicing skills essential to good communication. Some of these skills are outlined below.

Send a clear message

Don't expect her to be able to read your mind. Formulate what you are trying to communicate into words and tell her what is on your mind.

Don't send double messages. Your actions, facial expression, tone of voice, and body language all work together to communicate a message. If your words say one thing and your non-verbal cues say something else, there will be confusion.

Get through to her

Be aware of her receptivity at a given moment. If you know she is distracted, preoccupied, exhausted, or if children are vying for her attention, wait until a more opportune time.

Be aware of the emotional climate. Try to find a time to communicate when both of you are calm. In situations where emotions flare whenever an important message becomes the topic of conversation, consider putting your message into writing and leaving it for her to receive.

Listen

Don't interrupt. Listen to what she is saying and keep listening until she is satisfied her message has been sent. You can respond with your comments once she is finished.

Maintain eye contact. Let her know you are with her by looking her in the eye as she talks.

Don't focus your attention on preparing your rebuttal while she is still talking. Focus on trying to understand clearly what she is saying.

Listen to the feelings beneath the words. Take note of her non-verbal cues. If the words don't match the body language, tone of voice, and facial expression, ask yourself what feelings might be beneath the words.

Don't assume anything! Once you have asked yourself what she really might mean, don't assume your theory to be true. Instead, ask questions that will reveal what really is being said.

Give and receive feedback

Give non-verbal cues to let her know you are focused on her. A nod of the head or an empathetic smile can tell her you are listening.

Reflect on what you thought you heard her say and ask if you understood her correctly. This will give her a chance to clarify her meaning.

Keep asking questions until what you think you heard is the same as what she was trying to get across. Ask questions beginning with phrases like, "Do I understand you to mean . . . ?" "Are you trying to say . . . ?" "Can you explain more clearly the part about . . . ?"

When trying to send her a message, openly receive the feedback she gives you. Listen when she tells you what she thought she heard you say. Clarify your meaning. Answer her questions without allowing defensiveness to block communication.

PERSONAL EVALUATION

- Have you experienced frustration at times when it seemed you and your wife were approaching a conversation from two contrasting views of the world?
- Do you think your communication in marriage could be enriched by educating yourself about the differing communication styles used by men and women?
- Are you willing to learn and practice the skills that lead to good communication?

ACTION

Rate yourself on a scale of one to ten for how well you perform in the use of the four basic communication skills noted above (one is poor; ten is excellent). Next, have your wife read this day's journey and ask her to rate you. Compare your scores. The chances are that your scores will not be identical. Together practice the tips given for good communication until each of you clearly understands why the other rated your communication skills as they did. The goal is to understand why she rated you as she did and to practice your communication skills, not to change her mind. Remember the differing frames of reference and discuss how these influence the quality of communication between you.

REFLECTION

Consider how the ability to maintain good communication affects every aspect of married life. How could improving your ability to understand your mate, and be understood by her, enhance other facets of your marriage?

ENCOURAGEMENT

If you are willing to practice, you can master the skills that lead to good communication. When you polish these skills, you will benefit in your marriage, in other family relationships, in social settings, and in work relationships.

FOOD FOR THOUGHT

The first duty of love is to listen.
—Paul Tillich

Confront Problems Honestly and Hopefully

A great husband doesn't pretend there are no problems; he confronts problems honestly and deals with them in positive ways. You have your problems, your wife has hers, and there are some problems you share. When you learn to face all problems with hope that they can be overcome, you will be a better husband.

Every woman needs someone to help her keep a realistic perspective. There will be times your wife will have problems that seem insurmountable, problems she is trying to ignore or deny. You do her no favors by allowing her to live in a fantasy world. Denial can be deadly if the problems are allowed to compound. Whenever you are aware your wife has a problem, even if she is in denial, you need to give her the gift of a loving confrontation. If you go along with her pretense, you are abdicating your protective role in her life and will share responsibility for whatever pain comes. You are responsible to confront her honestly and not spare her the consequences that result from untended problems. If you pretend there isn't a problem, she might lack motivation to deal with the problem.

You should rely on your wife to help you see past your blind spots in recognizing and dealing with your own problems. In marriage, a personal problem can quickly turn into a marriage problem. When your life is in union with your wife, she will experience the effects of problems in your life that are denied. Your wife can give you support and encouragement in dealing with your problems, but you must make the ultimate decision to face them and get whatever help is necessary. When you learn to identify, face, and solve your personal problems, you will feel better about yourself, feel less defensive in relationship with your wife, and be free to be your best.

There is one problem which may make it extremely difficult to deal with all other problems of a personal nature. This is dealing with unhealthy shame. Unhealthy shame is the deeply rooted belief you are a flawed human being, that there is something wrong with you that can't be changed and must be hidden. When unhealthy shame is at the foundation of your self-image, you will avoid, hide, or run from all problems because you don't believe there is a solution. Rather, you see problems as evidence of your flawed nature and fear being exposed and rejected. If you think you may be dealing with issues related to unhealthy shame, get help dealing with those before trying to focus on other problems. Once you are free from the grip of unhealthy shame you will have the hope necessary to begin facing and resolving other personal problems.

PERSONAL EVALUATION

- Are you able to deal with problems honestly with the hope that any problem can be solved?
- Have you learned good problem-solving skills?

- If not, are you willing to educate yourself and learn the process for solving problems?
- Do you ignore your wife's problems and shield her from the natural consequences resulting from untended personal problems? If so, why?

ACTION

List five personal problems you have.

List five personal problems your wife has.

List five problems you and your wife share.

Next to each one place a *C* if the problem is being confronted in some positive way; place a *D* if the problem is being denied by someone and write the name/s of who is in denial; place a question mark if the problem is recognized, but you and your wife are not sure what to do.

Plan some time to talk with your wife about how the two of you can learn to deal with problems in your lives. Ask her to tell you which of your personal problems concern her most. Listen to see if she may be able to see problems in your life that you may need to face and deal with. Tell her about the problems you see in her life that concern you, and offer to help her resolve them.

Choose one of your personal problems that needs attention and work on finding a solution. Once you have that one solved, go back to the list and tackle another one.

REFLECTION

How do you feel dealing with problems? Do you have confidence you can find a solution? Think of all the problems you have successfully solved in your lifetime; what was the common process involved?

ENCOURAGEMENT

You can solve your problems if you are willing to face them honestly, and get the help you need.

FOOD FOR THOUGHT

Confrontation doesn't always bring a solution to the problem, but until you confront the problem there will be no solution.

—James Baldwin

Give Yourself (and Her) Some Time

Being a great husband takes more than desire; it also takes time. You can't be a great husband if you don't take time for refreshing yourself, time to love your wife, time to learn and practice skills that will make you a great partner. You also need to give yourself time to be patient with yourself. Don't demand overnight success with the changes you want to make. Changing habits and patterns may not be easy or instantaneous.

Now is the time in your journey to re-think the distribution of time under your control. The use of your time says a great deal about your real priorities. You can say you want to be a great husband, but if you continue to live your life with other commitments keeping you from spending time with your wife, your words will ring hollow. You probably have tremendous demands on your time, many of which involve things you do to make a living so you can provide for your family. The use of your time in this way can be a valid demonstration of love. However, it is never a substitute for a relationship where love is being expressed one to one.

PERSONAL EVALUATION

- Does your current schedule reflect the time you want to spend being your best, loving your wife, and partnering with her in life?

- Are there commitments you have taken on yourself that interfere with being a great husband, which could be delegated to others?
- Are you willing to make some scheduling changes to enhance your marriage and allow yourself the time it takes to be a great husband?

ACTION

Chronicle your plans for the next two weeks. Your goal is to mold your real schedule to fit the shape of your true values, especially your desire to be a great husband.

Step One: Sketch out a diagram that depicts 24 hours for each day in the coming two weeks. If you already keep a calendar, you will need to refer to the plans you have recorded already.

Step Two: Fill in the hours you regularly spend sleeping, eating, grooming, and taking care of other necessities.

Step Three: Fill in the hours already committed to ongoing activities that you are not in a position to change, such as school, work, church, and so on.

Step Four: Fill in all of the appointments you have planned for the next two weeks, such as going to the dentist or attending meetings, sporting events, or social events.

Anything left open on your calendar should represent areas of opportunity: opportunities to work at being your best, to love your wife, and to move in the direction of being a better life partner. Also consider whether any of your appointments might be optional when weighed against your desire to find time to be a great husband.

Step Five: Make a list of the things that you would like to do that fit into the three categories of being a great husband.

Step Six: Schedule in at least one hour daily for taking care of yourself in the particular ways you have chosen. Schedule in specific times each day for showing love to your wife in some of the ways you have chosen. Arrange with your wife to schedule a date for one evening each week. Schedule time each week for working on developing the knowledge and skills you will soon identify for your long-term goals of being a great partner.

Step Seven: Look back at the lists of things you chose to do in step five and *schedule them into your daily calendar as appointments*. If they do not fit into appointed times, *commit them to a specific day*.

This commitment should be realistic or you will become discouraged. A small improvement, which is within reach, is better than an idealistic calendar, which will prove overwhelming.

REFLECTION

Are you excited about whatever changes you are able to make, or are you feeling guilty that you can't do more?

ENCOURAGEMENT

Remember, changing your schedule is a major undertaking. Whatever positive changes you commit yourself to, and follow through on, will make a positive difference as they are repeated over the course of days, months, and years.

FOOD FOR THOUGHT

With the high value placed on time, giving your wife the time of day shows how valuable your relationship with her truly is.

Plan to Stay in Touch

Have you ever had the feeling your wife was more like a roommate than an intimate life partner? Do you find sometimes weeks will go by without having a chance for a heart-to-heart talk with your wife? Does she sometimes complain because your schedules conflict, she feels neglected, or has trouble getting your attention? Many families struggle to stay connected, given the host of conflicting options vying for everyone's attention. You may live under the same roof, share the same bed, be parents to the same children, while losing touch with one another as you each race to fulfill individual commitments and aspirations.

Staying in touch with your wife doesn't just happen. You have to plan to stay in touch. You must choose to agree about schedules, family business, and common goals. You must take time to communicate how each of you is feeling, to fight your battles together, to celebrate your victories, to provide support one for another. If you do not plan to stay in touch, the swift currents of daily events can pull you apart before you realize what is happening.

Dr. Charlie Shedd recommends at least fifteen minutes of heart-to-heart conversation between husband and wife each day to prevent this type of relational drift. This should be meaningful conversation, not just an account of the day's events and discussions of what is needed from the grocery store.

These should be times to sit quietly together, look into one another's eyes, and share what is going on inside you. He also recommends a weekly night out alone together to enjoy one another and nurture romance.

The family meeting can also provide a format that will serve to keep you in touch. Even if your family consists only of you and your wife, you can benefit from having regular family meetings without these times having to be formal and awkward. If you have children, you and your wife will be able to use these meetings to listen to your children's input, hear complaints, resolve conflicts, coordinate plans, correct wrong conduct, clarify misunderstandings, affirm your children, demonstrate parental unity, and highlight areas of family policy.

You will also be able to see where you may be getting off track and make revisions in your conduct. For example, during the discussion of what each one is involved with and what they need from the others in the family, you may hear a recurrent theme that your children and wife are needing more of your time or attention. This feedback can help you determine whether you are over-committed outside the home. Perhaps you need to reevaluate your commitments and draw back from some of them, or explain to your family the special circumstances that demand your attention away from home. The needs of your wife and children will not disappear. But you will be in a better position as a family to make decisions about how to fill those needs until you can get your schedule back under control.

An effective family meeting has the following elements: consistency, fun (perhaps special refreshments), time for each person to contribute and be heard, a summary of what was discussed and decided, and follow-up from the previous meeting to make sure that what was decided has been complied with.

Family meetings should be held at regular intervals, such as weekly and monthly. In addition, there can be meetings held for special purposes, such as responding to a family emergency or preparing for the holiday season. Each person can share in the process by taking turns helping with refreshments, being asked what they have to say, and being held accountable for following through on what has been asked of them. Each family member should be allowed to bring any topic to the family meeting. Someone can be designated to take notes on what is decided and what is to be done by whom, in response to decisions made during the meeting. These notes can be a tool to help each member communicate and stay connected to the overall goals of the family.

PERSONAL EVALUATION

- Are you willing to take the lead in arranging to have fifteen minutes of heart-to-heart conversation with your wife each day?
- Are you willing to plan a date alone with your wife to keep the romance alive in your marriage?
- What do you currently do to ensure ongoing communication and cooperation within your family?
- What hesitations do you have about putting these plans into action? Examine each one and

ask yourself if the obstacles outweigh the potential good?

ACTION

Take fifteen minutes to sit down with your wife and have a heart-to-heart conversation.

Ask your wife out for a date this week and make plans to have time with her that is both fun and romantic.

Plan and hold a family meeting. Explain to your wife (and children if you have them) that you have been taking a journey and this is your assignment. Your children may complain, but if you can share your enthusiasm and sell them on the benefits, they may be excited about the idea. Be sure you have the meeting well planned, so they know what to expect. Keep the meeting brief enough, and each member involved enough, so the children don't get bored. The day before the meeting, ask individually all family members if they have anything in particular they wish discussed at the family meeting. Record these for yourself as a checklist of topics to bring up.

Here is a sample format to follow. You can amend it as you see fit.

Introduction (three minutes): Go over why you want to have a meeting, any special topics on the agenda, and rules for how the meeting will be conducted.

Rules:
1. Everyone will get a chance to talk.
2. Listen when others talk.
3. Don't be afraid to bring up what is important to

you. (Let them know that you will make sure no one is disregarded or ridiculed.)

Schedule for the week (ten minutes): Discuss what is happening that needs attention (special events, after-school activities, working late). Is the calendar planned so that family members get where they need to be at the time they need to be there?

Update (ten minutes): Have each family member tell what is going on in his or her life and any ways the rest of the family can help.

Feelings (ten to twenty minutes): Have each family member tell one thing that made them feel good (happy, proud, excited), one thing that made them feel uncomfortable (angry, sad, worried, afraid), and one funny thing that happened to them or that they heard during the last week. As the director, be sure to keep everyone focused on the person who is sharing feelings. This helps affirm each person.

Problems or complaints (ten to twenty minutes): Allow each person to be heard; then facilitate discussion of possible solutions. It's your job to lead the discussion, maintain order, summarize solutions, and give direction.

Appreciation: Have each person say one thing he or she noticed and appreciated in the life of another family member that week.

Special topics: Discuss any special topics you have.

Summary: Have the designated person summarize the major decisions that were made and who is responsible to take action in the coming week. This can also include who will plan refreshments for the next meeting. (Note: Your children will be more highly motivated to participate if the meeting is associated with some small, special treat given at the meeting.)

REFLECTION

How has planning to stay in touch affected your relationship with your wife?

How did the family meeting go? If you were to continue having these meetings on a regular basis, what benefits do you anticipate? What changes would you make for future meetings? What skills do you want to develop to become better able to facilitate this kind of meeting? Are you willing to continue having family meetings for six weeks to see how it goes? What did you learn that was news to you?

ENCOURAGEMENT

You may not feel completely comfortable with planning to stay in touch. By doing so, even if you don't feel comfortable with the process, your wife will see your interest in her and you will be protecting against your lives drifting apart.

FOOD FOR THOUGHT

The art of progress is to preserve order amid change and to preserve change amid order.
—Alfred North Whitehead

Characteristics of a Great Partner

Marriage is much more than a relationship of love; it is also a partnership for life. Consider this poem by Robert Frost, which became the inscription on the gravestone above the grave where he and his wife Elinor were buried:

> Two such as you with such a master speed,
> Cannot be parted nor be swept away
> From one another once you are agreed
> That life is only life forevermore
> Together wing to wing and oar to oar.

What a beautiful monument to their lifetime partnership!

Within these verses are also some clues to how you can be a great life partner. Let's start with them and continue looking at other things you can do to make the most of your lifetime partnership.

Agree in your heart that life together is life forevermore. Don't allow yourself to see your commitment in marriage as anything less than love for a lifetime.

Fly wing to wing. Face the changing winds of life together, heading in the same direction. Don't turn against each other.

Agree on common purposes and goals. Once you know what your shared purposes and goals are, you can make independent decisions that support your common aim.

Major on your strengths and allow your wife to major on hers. Each of you has your particular strong and weak points. Work together to find ways that each person's strengths are used to the maximum good of both.

Complement your wife at her points of weakness. Instead of tearing her down where she is weak, look to see what you can do to support her. Help lift her up until she can grow stronger. If there is some area where she is weak and you are strong, design your functions within the relationship so you cover that area. She can do the same for you.

Agree to disagree. When you agree on the major issues, you can agree to disagree on minor points.

Share your wisdom with her. Your wife needs your perspective and input on all decisions that affect your family. Share your knowledge, your sensitivity to certain situations, your perceptions and opinions.

Never forget that you are on the same team. When you are aware of this, you will not seek to tear your wife down or compete against her.

PERSONAL EVALUATION

- Rate yourself on a scale of one to ten (one being poor; ten being excellent) for each of these characteristics of a great partner.
- What other characteristics for a great partner can you think of? Rate yourself on these as well.

ACTION

Reading over the list above, think of examples for each point where you have displayed a particular characteristic of a great partner.

List things you feel you need to do, or characteristics you need to develop, to become a better partner in life.

Write a description of shared purposes for your life together. You may want to discuss this with her first.

List the specific goals you and your wife share spiritually, economically, sexually, socially.

REFLECTION

When you and your wife have passed away, what would you want your epitaph to reflect about your lifelong marriage?

When thinking about marriage lasting a lifetime, do you have reasons to fear that yours may not last that long? What can you do to change things so those fears become unfounded?

ENCOURAGEMENT

The number of marriages that don't make it are often the focus of attention. There are plenty of marriages that do last a lifetime, and yours can be one of them.

FOOD FOR THOUGHT

To keep the fire burning brightly there's one easy rule: keep the two logs together, near enough to keep each other warm and far enough apart—about a finger's breadth—for breathing room. Good fire, good marriage—same rule.

—Marnie Reed Crowell

Being a Great Sexual Partner

Since you and your wife have made the commitment to keep yourselves exclusively for one another as sexual partners, it is important to be a great sexual partner. This is not to say that you should do anything you are not comfortable with in an attempt to keep your wife from looking elsewhere. It does mean sexuality is an important part of your being, and sexual fulfillment within marriage needs to be nurtured.

Here are some ways you can be a great sexual partner:

Take care of your self-esteem. When you are feeling good about yourself, you will be more comfortable with sexual intimacy. Sex within marriage is intended to be a deep knowing of one another. If you feel badly about yourself, you won't have a desire to be known deeply. Get help for any problems that keep you from intimacy with your wife.

Get to know what you like sexually, and let your wife know. She can't read your mind. Tell your wife when she does something that gives you pleasure. Tell her the things you would like to try. If there are things she is doing you don't enjoy, talk about it. Learning to communicate your sexual needs and desires is important.

Get to know what she likes, and be generous in pleasing her. Ask her what she likes, notice her responses, become a student of what she enjoys, and practice giving her pleasure.

Get enough rest. You can't be a great sexual partner when you are exhausted. Taking care to get enough rest is a way of preparing to make love to your wife.

Be creative. Don't let sex become routine. Think of ways you can make sex new (change your surroundings, change your bedroom attire, change locations).

Educate yourself. You can learn to be a great sexual partner. Read books, magazine articles, and other materials that will help you educate yourself about human sexuality.

Get help for problems that interfere with a satisfying sex life. If you are experiencing problems that you don't know how to solve on your own, consider seeing a professional who could help identify the factors contributing to your lack of sexual satisfaction and deal with them. There is excellent help available. There is no reason for you or your wife to be deprived of sexual satisfaction in marriage when you can find help.

Guard your most powerful sexual organ: your mind. Pornography has been shown to be both addictive and destructive to sexual satisfaction within marriage. If you are addicted to pornography, or involved in other forms of sexual addiction, this will eventually have a detrimental effect on your level of sexual satisfaction in marriage. There are twelve-step groups as well as treatment programs designed specifically to help people break free of sexual addiction and redirect their energies into a healthy marriage relationship.

Plan time for intimacy. Don't expect great sex to just happen. Plan time for it, and then guard your time together.

PERSONAL EVALUATION

- Have you ever told your wife specifically what you enjoy sexually?
- Are you sure you know what she enjoys?
- What have you done to educate yourself about sexual enjoyment in marriage?
- What personal problems do you have that interfere with sexual intimacy? What are you doing to resolve them?
- If you use pornography, are you willing to consider the possible negative effects this can have on your ongoing ability to be a great sexual partner? If you secretly use pornography, how does guilt or conflict affect your intimacy? Are you willing to consider the addictive effects of pornography and consider giving it up to redirect your energies and affections toward your wife rather than your fantasies?

ACTION

Go to the library or bookstore and get a book to educate yourself on ways you can enrich your sex life.

Plan an evening or weekend alone with your wife when you can discuss how each of you is feeling about your sexual relationship. Share what you would like to see happen to enrich your own sex life, and listen to what your wife has to say about hers.

Check your calendar to make sure you have planned enough time for rest and intimate enjoyment of your wife.

REFLECTION

Think about a sexually satisfying encounter with your wife. Focus on how she would please you and how you would please her.

ENCOURAGEMENT

Giving attention to yourself as a sexual partner can bring new life to your marriage.

FOOD FOR THOUGHT

Meaningful touching outside the bedroom can light sparks in a marriage, and meaningful communication can fan the flames.

—Gary Smalley

Being a Great Partner in Building Home and Family

According to Josiah G. Holland in *Gold Foil: Home,* "Home, in one form or another, is the great object of life." As a husband, you have the power and privilege to help create a home. With a little imagination and planning, your home can be a place toward which your family and friends gravitate. You may think the key to making your home a great place to be is to have all the latest gadgets and gizmos, the pool, and the big-screen TV. All of those amenities might be nice, but the most important elements, which make your home the place to be, are not things you can purchase.

If you have children, you can help design your home to become the place in your neighborhood where your children and their friends want to be whenever they have the choice. There is a growing hunger among youth today to have a place where they are known and loved, a place where they are not an interruption; a place where they don't get the message that they are in the way. Your attitude sets the tone for this kind of atmosphere.

It is important to negotiate a reasonable division of labor to keep your home in order. Depending on your situation and the values your family holds, you will work out some sort of arrangement to keep domestic life manageable. Each member of your family can do something to contribute to keeping your home running smoothly, if they have a plan to follow, instructions on how to do what is asked of them, and some form of motivation. You can provide leadership in partnering with your wife to manage your home and train your children to participate in these family responsibilities.

An important part of being a great partner in building your family is making sure you have made a clean break from your parents. The Bible says, "A man shall leave his father and mother and cleave to his wife." Anytime a man fails to leave his childhood home, whether physically or emotionally, this will interfere with his ability to establish his own home. If you find yourself torn between pleasing your parents or pleasing your wife, there is cause for concern.

If you have children, being a great husband involves learning to be a good father and building relationships with your children. As with any other role and responsibility, you will need to learn to parent. Your willingness to love your children and learn the skills to be a good father will knit your heart together with your wife as you partner together in parenting. This is equally important if you have stepchildren. A man's love for his wife's children goes a long way in demonstrating love to her.

PERSONAL EVALUATION

- What do you do to build the success of your home and family?
- Do you feel like you are in partnership with your wife to build the home and family, or have you left her alone in carrying these responsibilities?

- Have you ever used your creative imagination to dream up the kind of home you are trying to create for your family?
- What areas of knowledge or ability do you lack, which keep you from building your home and family the way you would like?
- Are you certain you have completely left your father and mother in order to establish your own home and family?

ACTION

Rate yourself on a scale of one to ten (one being poor; ten being excellent) on the following:

- Your attitude helps make the atmosphere of your home pleasant and inviting.
- Your home is a place your children and their friends want to be.
- You have negotiated a reasonable division of labor to keep your home in order.
- You provide leadership in managing your home.
- You participate in training your children to share in the family responsibilities of keeping your home in order.
- You are learning to be a good father.
- You spend time building relationships with your children.
- If you have stepchildren, you are learning to be a good father to them and are trying to build relationships.

Look over your ratings and decide what you would like to do to become a better partner in building the kind of home and family you would like to have. From these, list three things you could learn to help you increase your knowledge of managing your home. List three things you could do to develop skills needed to build up your home and family. List three ways you could help your wife be better able to help manage your home.

Set one long-range goal to improve your ability to be a great partner in building a home and family. Write it down, and plan how you could achieve it in the next six months.

REFLECTION

Envision your home as you would like it to be. Consider how you can manage the financial resources and human resources around you to make that vision a reality.

ENCOURAGEMENT

Being a great husband is a foundation of a successful home and family. Your efforts have far-reaching effects.

FOOD FOR THOUGHT

To be sure, working—that is, earning a living—is one aspect of fathering. It's one means that the father has of extending protection to the family. But it's just one. If he concentrates on this to the exclusion of other aspects it becomes not a form of fathering, but an escape.

—Myron Brenton

Being a Great Spiritual Partner

Human beings are made in the image of God, body, mind, and spirit. When you enter into the union of marriage, there is a spiritual union as well as a physical one. When you and your wife share a common faith in God and similar spiritual experiences, this can be a very rich part of your marriage. When you do not share a common faith or spiritual understanding, this can bring added tension to the relationship. Whatever your particular situation, here are some guidelines to help you consider how you can be a great spiritual partner within your marriage.

Seek God. Draw close to God and allow your relationship with God to enrich your life. Develop the qualities of true spirituality: humility, love, generosity, faith, courage, strength, and serenity. These enrich all of life.

Allow the richness of what your faith brings to you to overflow in love for your wife.

Pray for your wife. Regardless of your wife's own spiritual experience, you are always free to pray for her. Pray for her well-being, her work, her health, for blessings in her life. Pray about everything that concerns her.

Sincerely seek to understand what she believes and why. Try to understand the influences that have shaped her spiritual experience.

Never allow yourself to become self-righteous or

condescending toward her if she doesn't share your beliefs or spiritual experience.

As the head of your home you have a unique responsibility to convey spiritual truth and an understanding of God to the next generation of your family. If you have a healthy relationship with God that is fulfilling your spiritual needs, you are called to share your knowledge of God and love for Him with your children, telling them about all the wonderful things God has done for you. If you do not have a healthy relationship with God or are not sure of your relationship with Him, it will be difficult for you to fulfill your calling to spiritual leadership within your family. God is eager to equip you to be the spiritual leader of your family. If this is something you desire, or would be willing for God to do through you, ask Him to lead you in that direction. Then begin actively pursuing a personal relationship with God. It is not enough for you to send your children to church; you need to lead them there.

PERSONAL EVALUATION

- How would you describe the spiritual aspect of your life?
- How do your beliefs about God affect your family relationships?
- Do you know what your wife believes and what influences have shaped those beliefs?
- What can you do with your wife that might enrich your lives spiritually?
- If you are not experiencing a healthy spiritual life, are you willing to pursue a relationship with God? If not, what holds you back?

ACTION

Pray for your own spiritual enrichment. Pray for your wife, and pray for God's help to become the best husband you can possibly be.

If you are not accustomed to praying, don't worry. Just talk to God as though He were a friend sitting with you and wanting to know what is on your heart and mind. If you prefer, you can write your prayer in the form of a letter to God.

REFLECTION

What are you doing that displays spiritual leadership of your family? Are you experiencing a desire for a greater sense of meaning in your life? Consider how you and your wife could partner together to enrich your spiritual lives.

ENCOURAGEMENT

Seek God. The Bible promises that everyone who seeks God with a sincere heart will find Him. When you do, whether it's for the first time or for a fresh touch of His hand, your life will be enriched. When you take over spiritual leadership of your family, every member of your family will benefit.

FOOD FOR THOUGHT

God says, "And you will seek Me and find Me, when you search for Me with all your heart."
—Jeremiah 29:13

Being a Great Economic Partner

Work and money play a central role in the way you live your life. They are also often at the center of marital conflict. When your life is united in marriage, you are an economic partner with your wife. In the book *Partners In Love*, Alanson B. Houghton has this to say: "Money is so central to our daily economic and emotional well-being that partners, especially marriage partners, must understand its dynamics and how the other feels about money."

In our society, the changing economic climate is having a tremendous impact on marriage and the family. Being able to juggle these responsibilities while balancing your life and nurturing your marriage is no easy task. Whatever your economic circumstances, there are trade-offs that will test the confidence you have in your choices regarding where your time and energy are being expended. In these economic realities of life, it is most important that you and your wife work out shared priorities and goals.

A great husband will work toward providing financial security for his family. Your wife may enjoy working outside the home and pursuing a career. However, if she is forced to work outside the home because you are not providing financially, this creates great stress. This is especially true if she would prefer to stay home to care for her children, but is unable to do so for economic reasons. If you are working as hard as you can and are still unable to provide for your family's basic needs, consider what action you can take so that, in time, your wife will enjoy the freedom to pursue a career or enjoy the freedom to focus her energies solely on home and family, if that is her desire.

Consider the following things you can do to be a great economic partner.

Discuss, clarify, and agree on family priorities related to finances. Make plans to adjust your family budget and your career to free your wife to choose whether or not to work outside the home.

It is important to plan for the future together with your wife regarding each one's life work. You each have aspirations and concerns about what you want to accomplish and achieve. Take time to communicate about what she wants her life's work to be and what you want your life's work to be. Help her plan for a future that moves toward the kind of work she wants to do and ask for her help in doing the same, while both of you make sure the needs of your minor children are a top priority.

Discuss and agree on financial goals for spending, earnings, saving, investing, and budgeting.

Communicate with your wife so that you both know what your budget is, your net worth, information regarding insurance policies, investments, and the like. Think through financial decisions with your wife.

Educate yourself in areas of finance and economics.

Do your best to make your financial resources go as far as possible. Learn to make the most of your money by reducing debts, spending wisely, and learning to live in ways that do not waste the money you have at your disposal.

PERSONAL EVALUATION

- Are you and your wife agreed on priorities for childcare, work outside the home for each of you, and time together?
- Do you understand how your wife feels about money, working outside the home, or staying home to care for your children? How does she feel about the economic changes taking place in the world today?
- Are you feeling threatened by changing societal roles?
- Do you feel confident as a partner in the economic area of life with your wife? Do you bear the responsibility for family finances, or do you leave these burdens for your wife to deal with on her own?
- Are you willing to work toward adjusting your career goals and life-style so that you can provide for your family's basic needs?
- What problems in your marriage relate to financial or work-related matters?
- Can you see how becoming better informed and educated on economic matters could help strengthen your marriage partnership?

ACTION

Cite one area of conflict related to family economics. Consider what you could do to become a better economic partner to help resolve the conflict.

Set a specific goal to learn something new that would help you deal with the issues related to the problem. Set a goal of what you can do in the next six months to help resolve this conflict by being a better economic partner.

If you and your wife are not clearly agreed on your family priorities related to work and childcare, discuss these issues and set your priorities together.

REFLECTION

How do your feelings about work and money affect your marriage?

ENCOURAGEMENT

You can learn the things you need to know to become a great economic partner. When your finances are in order, it will help your home be in order.

FOOD FOR THOUGHT

Life is work, and everything you do is so much more experience. Sometimes you work for wages, sometimes not, but what does anybody make but a living? And whatever you have you must use or lose.

—Henry Ford

Promote a Policy of Reaching Out

"Peter, Peter, Pumpkin Eater had a wife and couldn't keep her. He put her in a pumpkin shell and there he kept her very well." What worked in this nursery rhyme would never work in a real marriage.

To maintain a healthy marriage you must encourage a policy of reaching out in appropriate ways. Your wife has needs that are best met through relationship with other women. There are many needs you have that will be filled by developing healthy relationships with other men. Individually, each of you will have times when you face problems that need help beyond that which the other can supply. By promoting a policy of reaching out for appropriate help, you will enable yourself and your wife to overcome personal problems that affect the marriage. Additionally, the two of you will find your lives enriched by reaching out together to experience new things and to help others in your community.

Here are some ways you can promote a policy of reaching out:

Encourage your wife to develop a network of supportive relationships with other women. You can be her best friend, but you cannot be expected to fill the same role played by her best girlfriend in high school. A woman's relationship with other women is unique and can fill needs a man can never meet.

Some men discourage their wives from attending women's groups or social activities because they are concerned that these relationships may draw her away from her family. Usually, by being involved with other women, especially in groups that are supportive of family values, the woman comes back to her family relationships refreshed, encouraged, and more energized to fulfill her roles within the family. If you see your family as a closed system, where you are afraid for your wife to develop relationships with others, this may be an indication that there is a need for trust that will allow you to feel comfortable with her reaching out to others.

Build healthy relationships with other men who share a commitment to building up their families. Men need relationships with other men. Whether this is in a recreational setting like sports, or in a men's prayer group, you can benefit from these relationships. It is important to note that your fulfillment of your role as a husband can also be damaged if you spend time with men who don't have respect for the values that will build up your marriage and family life. If you are stopping off at the local pub with your old buddies who are living lives opposed to that which builds a healthy marriage, you cannot help but be negatively affected. Bad company corrupts good morals. Make sure the men you choose to associate with will encourage you to be a great husband.

Be willing to reach out for help whenever there is a problem bigger than both of you. Being a great husband and leader of your family doesn't mean you have to have all the answers. Any good leader knows the value of reaching out for the best help or knowledge available when there is a problem they are unprepared to solve on their own. There is no shame in admitting need and getting whatever help is necessary to deal with the difficulties of life, whether those are physical, relational, emotional, spiritual, or financial.

Reach out to new experiences together. Think of ways you can share reaching out to help others. Volunteer together for a community organization or offer to work with the youth group at your church. What do you and your wife do together that is new and exciting? Think of ways the two of you can learn new things together. Perhaps take a class together, learn to dance, learn more about one of your wife's interests, or share one of your interests with her.

PERSONAL EVALUATION

- Do you encourage your wife's involvement in a network of supportive women friends?
- Do you reach out to develop healthy relationships with other men, who encourage your fulfillment of your family roles and responsibilities?
- Are you open to reaching out for help with family problems when you are not equipped to handle them on your own?
- What do you and your wife do together that takes you beyond the relationships in your family to build relationships with others in your community?

ACTION

Talk with your wife about which of her needs are going unmet. Together consider how she might reach out to other women in ways that would help fulfill some of these needs.

If you are not involved in healthy relationships with other men, do some research to find groups or organizations of men where you can develop some new relationships. If you are interested in resources for men, you can contact Focus On The Family at (719) 531-5181. Check with your local church, chamber of commerce, or other civic organizations where you could get involved in healthy relationships with other men. Once you find a group or activity that interests you, make time in your schedule to develop these relationships.

Identify any problems that are unresolved in your family. Take decisive action to reach out for the help your family needs.

Choose one activity you and your wife can do together to reach out to your community, either in volunteer service or in shared experience with others. Then reach out to your community together. Keep trying things until you find an activity that you both enjoy.

REFLECTION

Sometimes it feels uncomfortable to reach beyond the familiar relationships at home. What makes you feel uncomfortable about reaching out and about encouraging your wife and family to do the same? Can you see benefits of reaching out that can push you beyond your comfort level for the sake of enriching your family life?

ENCOURAGEMENT

Your willingness to promote a policy of reaching out will benefit your family in ways you alone cannot. Give them the gift of encouraging them to reach out to their world and bring back home that which has enriched their lives.

Continuing to Be a Great Husband

We have defined being a great husband to mean balancing your resources and abilities in each of three areas: being your best, knowing and loving your wife, and being a great partner in life. As you continue to keep this kind of healthy balance, you can live with the confidence that you are being a great husband.

You have already taken decisive action to plan ways to improve in each area. You have a notebook with short-term and long-term goals for each area. Why stop now? Each time you achieve one goal in each area, choose another to replace it. In this way you will continue to grow and find a sense of confidence that comes from knowing you are continuing to move in the right direction.

Your journey continues throughout your life. The important thing in continuing to be a great husband is not to lose momentum. Each day, one day at a time, keep your dreams clearly in sight and goals well defined, your tasks identified and obstacles targeted, and your relationship with your wife well nourished. The only way to do this is to plan and guard time for reflection.

Your life is divided into days, weeks, months, and years. At each of these segments of life you can ensure being a great husband by planning time for reviewing your life and revising your choices. To stay current with the changes life brings and continue being a great husband, plan for the following:

Daily quiet time. Give yourself some time and space each day to reflect on your life. Pray for wisdom and strength. Read nourishing materials. Think about what you are facing and how you can best attack the challenges of the day without compromising your priorities in life. Refresh your positive attitude. Give thanks for all that you have: your health, your family, the opportunities for growth.

Plan for weekly rest and reflection. One day each week, relieve yourself of the burden of work. Take this time to enjoy relationships with your family—play together, worship God together, enjoy one another's company. On your weekly day of rest, consider how well you did the previous week in your role as a husband. Consider what the week held for your wife and what she might need from you in the coming week. During your weekly checkup, examine how well you are nourishing yourself so that you can be your best, how well you are loving your wife and partnering together in facing what life has brought that week. You can take note of where you may be getting out of balance and make corrections before major problems have time to develop.

Your weekly self checkup should include considering how much quality time you have shared with your wife that week. Take note of whether you have made room for your daily heart-to-heart chats and your weekly date.

Plan caring for yourself as a husband into your monthly calendar. As you do whatever form of planning you do for each coming month, plan ways to enrich your marriage. Having a weekend away with your wife can be a romantic boost to your marriage. These marriage enrichment times will not happen by accident; you have to plan for them.

Plan for annual reviews. In the week between Christmas and New Year's Eve, take time to review your goals for life. Keep a notebook with all your goals in writing: family goals, financial goals, social goals, educational goals, spiritual goals, career goals, and so on. Look to see what goals you have accomplished in the past year. Revise your written goals for each area by listing immediate changes you want to make, short-term goals, one-year goals, five-year goals, and twenty-five-year goals. You will be amazed at how writing your goals down and reviewing them on an annual basis can keep you from growing stagnant. Including your goals for being a great husband will keep your marriage from growing stagnant too.

PERSONAL EVALUATION

- After taking your journey, do you have a sense of balance in all three areas? Are you taking clearly defined steps and making commitments to achieve balance in all three areas? Are you ready to see yourself as a great husband?
- Do you currently take daily quiet time, a weekly day of rest, times to plan your monthly calendar, and annual times for revising your old goals and setting new ones?
- If not, can you see enough value in doing so to motivate yourself to make these changes?

ACTION

Decide if you will continue to use your personal growth notebook to record and monitor your progress on the goals you set in terms of being your best, knowing and loving your wife, and partnering with her in life.

REFLECTION

How does taking charge of planning time for reflection, reviews, and revisions help you gain confidence that you can continue to be a great husband?

ENCOURAGEMENT

Your willingness to weave your good intentions into the fabric of your days, weeks, months, and years will bring your desire to be a great husband into reality.

Give Yourself Credit and Decide Where You Go from Here

Although you have come to the end of this 30-day journey, your personal journey continues. Being a great husband is a continuing goal. Hopefully, you have come to recognize that you are able to be a great husband when you choose to be. You have identified some areas that need continued attention, but remember that every human relationship requires ongoing care.

PERSONAL EVALUATION

Give yourself the credit due you. In the commitment you signed at the beginning of this journey you promised, "I will not focus my attention on how far I fall short of being the ideal husband. I will focus my attention on moving forward from where I am today toward what I want to be." By participating in each day's journey, you have taken many steps toward being a great husband. Don't take those for granted. Take time to see the changes and appreciate what you have done to reach your desired goal.

ACTION

Look back at days six through twenty-one. Each of these focused attention on ways you could make immediate changes that would contribute to being a great husband. Consider all the small changes you have made. They all make a difference. Look at the topics for each day and list at least one specific thing you did to move in that direction. What did you do to:

- accept responsibility for your life?
- renew your wholehearted commitment?
- appreciate what you have to offer?
- take care of your health and appearance?
- prepare to lay down your life?
- dare to lead with love?
- dump the woman of your dreams and accept the real woman you married?
- be considerate, kind, and affectionate?
- water the seeds of greatness within her?
- recognize her work and give her recognition?
- go beyond her expectations?
- respond to the differences between you?
- practice forgiveness?
- practice good communication skills?
- confront problems honestly and hopefully?

In days twenty-two through twenty-eight you focused your attention on areas relating to more long-range goals. Look at each area and take note of at least one thing you do well in the areas of being a great partner in life.

- What personal qualities are your strengths in making you a great partner for life?
- What is one thing you have done to move toward being a great sexual partner?
- What is one thing you have done to move toward

being a great partner in building a home and family?

- What is one thing you have done to move toward being a great spiritual partner?
- What is one thing you have done to move toward being a great economic partner?
- What is one thing you have done to promote a policy of reaching out?

Don't overlook the progress you have made! Applaud yourself for the progress you have made and for the awareness you have developed in terms of where you need to improve. It takes courage to recognize areas of weakness, and to choose to get help to strengthen you in ways that will help you be a better husband.

Take stock of the areas where you have had the courage to see needed changes and commit yourself to seeking change through setting goals.

- What is the one area where you need to make the most progress in terms of being your best?
- What is the one area where you need to make the most progress in terms of knowing and/or loving your wife?
- What is the one area where you need to make the most progress in terms of becoming a better partner in life?

Choose to end this journey by turning those issues you recognize as areas of potential growth into specific goals for your future.

Give yourself a reward for your progress. One of the best rewards you could give yourself would be to acknowledge that you are a great husband and are getting better all the time. If your wife has taken note of your sincere efforts and progress, let her help you celebrate your success.

REFLECTION

Remember back on day two, when you had your wife write her definition of what it means to be a great husband? Now is the time to read it. Read her definition and decide if you fit the bill of what she has described. Consider whether you surpass it, or if you disagree with her definition. Read over your original definition. How has your definition changed in the process of taking this journey?

ENCOURAGEMENT

If you have completed this journey, you have displayed effort and love for yourself and your wife.

FOOD FOR THOUGHT

We cannot do everything at once, but we can do something at once.

—Calvin Coolidge

Sometimes problems are too difficult to handle alone on a 30-day journey. If you feel that you need additional help, please talk with one of the counselors at New Life Treatment Centers. The call is confidential and free.

1-800-NEW-LIFE